The Letter of James

Clayton K. Harrop

CONVENTION PRESS
NASHVILLE, TENNESSEE

© Copyright 1969 Convention Press
Nashville, Tennessee

ALL RIGHTS RESERVED
5132-04

CODE NUMBER: Church Study Course
*This book is number 3204 in subject area 2, courses
for Adults and Young People*

Library of Congress catalog card number: 73-77618
Printed in the United States of America
390. MY 69 R.R.D.

Contents

1.
Introduction
to the
Letter

"Count it all joy, my brethren, when you meet various trials."

"If any of you lacks wisdom, let him ask God . . . and it will be given him."

"God cannot be tempted with evil and he himself tempts no one."

•"Of his own will he brought us forth by the word of truth."

"Be doers of the word, and not hearers only."

"If any one thinks he is religious, and does not bridle his tongue . . . this man's religion is vain."

"If you show partiality, you commit sin."

"I by my works will show you my faith."

"Where jealousy and selfish ambition exist, there will be disorder and every vile practice."

"God opposes the proud, but gives grace to the humble."

"Be patient, therefore, brethren, until the coming of the Lord."
"Confess your sins to one another, and pray for one another."

These brief quotations (RSV) serve to illustrate the writing style of James and to focus on the forthright and down-to-earth instructions of the short letter. Exercising an economy of words and writing in excellent Greek, this New Testament author recorded some of the most concise—and disturbing—biblical material in our Bible. It is not difficult to determine what is meant by this short writing, but it is most difficult to evade its persistent searchlight of truth. To use a biblical metaphor, the letter of James is quick and powerful; it is indeed sharper than any two-edged sword. With its incisive truth it divides "asunder" the sham from the reality of practiced Christianity. In today's vernacular, James seems to be saying, "Practice what you preach!"

This book has something to say to us in the 1970's. We read it not for comfort, but for a challenge, for instruction in the truth.

The answers to questions concerning authorship, date, destination, and purpose of a book of the Bible are always interesting and of value. Sometimes they are of unusual importance because the answers go far in determining the understanding of the writings. Passages take on new and richer meaning when these questions are answered.

The letter of James is one of the writings where answers to these questions are not so vital as with some other books. The conclusions reached about these matters do not greatly change the interpretation of many passages in the letter. However, this information better prepares us to understand James and to apply his teachings to our circumstances.

AUTHOR

There are two widely-separated opinions concerning the authorship of this letter. Many interpreters feel the letter was written by James, the brother (really the half brother) of Jesus. Others believe that the letter was written by someone else at a considerably later time. This other person may have been named James, or he could have borne some other name. There are other opinions, but these are the only two which we will consider in this study.

Claims of the Letter

The letter itself does not give a clear answer to the question of authorship. The author merely identified himself as "James, a slave of God and the Lord Jesus Christ" (1:1).* He did not claim any distinction, honor, or title. He did not refer to himself as an apostle, as Paul frequently did in his writings and as we find in the letters of Peter. He did not call himself a brother of Jesus. The opening words are greatly similar to those of the letter of Jude: "Jude, a slave of Jesus Christ, and brother of James" (Jude 1).

At least three men by the name of James are mentioned in the New Testament. In addition to the brother of Jesus, there are James the son of Zebedee and James the son of Alphaeus. There is little support for either of these as the author of this letter. James the son of Zebedee was martyred by Agrippa I in A.D. 44 (Acts 12:2). It is quite likely that this letter was not written that early, although one manuscript of the tenth century has a subscript naming James the son of Zebedee as the author.

We know almost nothing about James the son of Alphaeus, and there seems to be no reason to suppose that he was the author of the letter of James. However, those who identify James the son of Alphaeus with James the brother of Jesus claim the son of Alphaeus wrote the letter. But this identification is undoubtedly incorrect. We can be confident that these were two separate persons, and it is unlikely that the son of Alphaeus was the author.

---

* *Unless otherwise indicated, all translations from the Greek New Testament will be the author's.*

The aforementioned facts would seem to point to the brother of Jesus as the author of the epistle in question. It is interesting that the author did not call himself an apostle. Certainly Paul seems to have given him that title (Gal. 1:19). It may be that James refrained from using the title because he was not an apostle in the same sense as the original twelve. It is also interesting that James did not claim for himself the honor of being the brother of Jesus, if this were the case. Some say he made no such claim because of his humility; others suggest that he did not want his authority to be based upon this relationship. If he had authority, it was because of his spiritual leadership and not because he was the brother of Jesus.

The contents of the letter do not clarify the authorship. Reputable scholars read the letter and come to completely opposite conclusions. Because there are no clear references in the letter to events in the earthly life of Jesus and little or no reference to his death and resurrection, many interpreters do not feel the brother of our Lord wrote this letter. Possibly a consideration of the purpose of the writing would explain the lack of these references, but such explanations still do not solve any of the problems regarding authorship. It is usually agreed that the writer was a Jew, because the letter is more Jewish than most other New Testament writings. Also, the author was obviously familiar with the teachings of Jesus, especially the Sermon on the Mount. At this point, it is clear that there seems to be nothing in the letter which would be contrary to what we know of James the brother of Jesus.

Reference by Early Christian Writers

The testimony of later Christian writers is of little help with regard to authorship. Origen (early third century) was the first writer to refer to this letter as being written by James the brother of Jesus. It is quite difficult to determine how much the letter was used by writers in the early Christian centuries. If there are traces of its usage in the second century, and this is quite doubtful, they are never exact quotations. The similarities appearing in early Christian writings are probably due to the different authors drawing from the same background of tradition. Furthermore, no reference is made to the letter by name, nor to its author. At best, we can conclude that the letter of James was in circulation in the second century.

That the letter of James did not appear among Christian writings until quite late can be explained on the basis of the contents of the letter. The practical matters in it did not lend themselves to later citation as did the more theological writings of Paul, Peter, and John.

A number of factors may appear to point to someone other than the brother of Jesus as the author. It is claimed that the conditions reflected in the letter are those of the late first century or early second century. Some of these conditions will be mentioned in the discussion of the date of the letter.

Factors Concerning Author's Skill and Associations

It is true that the author wrote in excellent Greek. Could a Galilean, reared in the humble surroundings of the home in Nazareth and who lived most of his life in Jerusalem, attain to such a standard of the Greek language? We cannot be sure. It may have been possible, but we do not know enough about the circumstances of the day to answer the question with confidence.

Another factor concerns the relationship of this letter to other New Testament writings. There appears to be some relationship to 1 Peter and certain of Paul's writings, as well as to the teachings of Jesus. We cannot be sure there is a literary relationship. If there is, did James use these other writings or did they use James's? Despite the arguments of many writers, it appears likely that the relationships can be explained better on the basis of a common background of material than on the basis of one writer copying from the other.

However, there are certain things which may indicate that the author was the brother of Jesus: He was quite familiar with the teachings of Jesus. He was a man in a position of great authority. There are indications that the letter was written very early. (See later discussion on date of book.) The letter fits with the character of James as we learn it from the New Testament and other sources.

Conclusion About Authorship

It appears that the weight of evidence supports the idea that James the brother of Jesus wrote the letter. Perhaps this can never be more than merely an opinion. If the reader should reach another conclusion, it will not greatly affect the interpretation of the letter. In this study we shall assume that the author was the brother of our Lord and the name James will be used throughout this writing to indicate the author.

INFORMATION ABOUT JAMES, THE BROTHER OF JESUS

There are few references in the Gospels to the family of Jesus. We are told that Jesus had four brothers, of whom one was named James, and more than one sister (Mark 6:3). While this is a subject that is much discussed, the New Testament implies that these were younger children of Joseph and Mary. Therefore, James actually was a half brother of Jesus. The writings of Mark and John indicate that Jesus' family was not sympathetic to his earthly ministry (Mark 3:31–35; John 7:1–9).

There is no evidence to indicate exactly when James became a follower of Jesus. Paul noted that a resurrection appearance was granted to James (1 Cor. 15:7). We know nothing about the circumstance of this appearance or whether James was a believer before it occurred. We do know that James, and the rest of the family, was present with the disciples from the time of the ascension (Acts 1:12-24). James took a prominent part in the life of the church in Jerusalem, and before many years he became the leader of that church (Acts 15:12-29; 21:17-26; Gal. 1:19; 2:9). It may be that his family relationship with Jesus aided James in becoming the leader of the church in Jerusalem. On the other hand, he was undoubtedly worthy of the position on the basis of his own spiritual qualifications. Beyond these references, nothing is said in the New Testament concerning the life and ministry of James.

Certain traditions concerning James have been preserved by later writers. These traditions do not agree exactly and, therefore, cannot be depended upon as though they were from the Bible. But they may give us some additional insight into the character and activity of James.

The earliest reference to him outside the New Testament is found in the writing of the Jewish historian Josephus in the last quarter of the first century. While certain statements concerning Jesus in his writings may be later Christian insertions, there does not seem to be any reason to question his statements about James. The testimony of Josephus is that James was brought to trial at the instigation of the high priest Annas during a time when there was no Roman governor. He was charged with breaking the law and was stoned to death. This would have occurred about A.D. 62 (*Antiquities of the Jews,* xx, ix, 197-203).

A Christian historian of the fourth century, Eusebius, quoted a very dramatic account of the life and death of James from Hegesippus, a writer of the second century. According to this account, James was called the Just. He was holy from birth, drinking no wine and eating no meat. He was pictured as completely fulfilling the Nazirite vow of the Old Testament. While this is possible, the additional statement that he was permitted to enter the Holy Place undoubtedly is not true since only the high priest was permitted to do this. This account states that James spent so much time kneeling in prayer that his knees became hard like a camel's. The Jews sought to have James persuade the people not to believe in Jesus. When James refused, according to Eusebius, they set him on the pinnacle of the Temple, threw him down, and stoned him while he prayed for their forgiveness. He was finally killed when someone hit him on the head with a club, and he was buried beside the Temple. According to Eusebius, this was immediately followed by the siege of the city by the Roman armies. Thus his death would have been in A.D. 66 (Eusebius, *Ecclesiastical History,* ii, 23).

This account probably contains later additions, although certain elements of truth can be found in it. It is likely that the picture of James as an ascetic and a just man is true. He probably spent much time in prayer. But the manner of his death is probably better pictured by Josephus than it is by Hegesippus. All we can learn of James from outside sources agrees with what we find in the letter which bears his name in the New Testament.

DATE

The problems of date and authorship are closely linked. If James the brother of Jesus was the writer of the letter, then it must have been written before A.D. 62. If someone else wrote the letter, it is quite likely that the date would be toward the close of the first century. Some would even place it in the second century.

If the traditional authorship is accepted, two dates are possible. The early date is before A.D. 50. The late date is near the close of James's life, about A.D. 60. It is very difficult to justify the latter suggestion. It seems clear that the letter must be dated very early or very late in the apostolic age. One of the chief reasons for this is the fact that there is no reference in this writing to the relationship between Jew and Gentile in the church. We know from Paul's writings that this problem was troubling the minds of vast numbers of Christians during the period between A.D. 50 and 60. It is seen in Galatians, Romans, and the Corinthian correspondence. It is difficult to imagine that anyone writing during this period to congregations that were primarily, if not entirely, Jewish could do so without at least hinting at the critical problem of the acceptance of Gentiles into the fellowships. Either this was written before the controversy became widespread (Acts 15) or after the passionate strife had died down, somewhere toward the end of the century.

There are several reasons for suggesting an early date for the letter. One is the absence of the question concerning the admission of Gentiles. In addition, the meeting place of the Christians is referred to as a synagogue (2:2, in the original Greek). So far as we know, at an early date Christians began to speak of their meeting places as churches. There seems to have been little formal organization in the churches. The only officials referred to are the elders. The teachers, while many, do not seem to have held formal and official office.

The problem the author was concerned with in the matter of faith and works seems quite different from that which concerned Paul. There is no indication that the author was familiar with Paul's statement of the case. If he had been, he would undoubtedly have expressed his position in a different way to avoid any possibility of misunderstanding. All of this would strengthen the case for a date prior to A.D. 50.

Some scholars feel that the situation pictured in 4:1–4 could not have prevailed so early and suggest this demands a much later date for the letter. However, we know that other surprising conditions prevailed in the earliest churches. We cannot be sure that such conditions could not have occurred as well in A.D. 50 as in A.D. 100. But there is still the problem "how as late as A.D.

100 a book like James could still be written. Here is a tract, large parts of which might have been found in the Old Testament. References to Jesus are rare and almost casual. There is no hint of the Crucifixion, the Atonement, the Resurrection, or of the equal status of Jesus with God his Father. There *is* reference to the second coming [5:7, and possibly 5:9]. There are no bishops or deacons, only elders [5:14]. The church gathering is still called a *synagogue*." [1]

Other writers point to these same omissions and claim that no early writing could omit these important ideas. Could any Christian writing of such an early date be penned that did not place emphasis on the messiahship of Jesus, especially a writing addressed to Jews? Of course, if the readers were already believers, this would remove any necessity for such an emphasis.

On the basis of all the evidence available, it seems best to this writer to date this letter about A.D. 45-48. If this is correct, it makes it the earliest New Testament writing. This adds considerable significance to it for our study.

DESTINATION

Relatively little can be said with confidence about the destination of the letter. It was addressed "to the twelve tribes who are in the Diaspora" (1:1). The Diaspora was the area outside of Palestine. For several centuries the Jews had been scattered throughout this area, sometimes forcibly and sometimes voluntarily. Jews were looked upon as ideal colonists, and their migration was frequently encouraged by the nations which ruled them.

This opening greeting gives the impression that the readers were Jewish by race. There is nothing in the letter which should cause this impression to be questioned. Yet we recognize that in 1 Peter a similar phrase, "the elect sojourners of the Diaspora,"

---

[1] R. R. Williams, THE LETTERS OF JOHN AND JAMES (New Rochelle, N. Y.: Cambridge University Press, 1965), p. 94.

is probably a broader reference that includes Gentile believers.

There is no clear-cut indication as to where these Jews lived. It is doubtful that the letter was intended for all Jewish believers everywhere. There are indications within the letter which imply that the author had particular people and particular situations in mind. One common idea is that the letter was written to Jewish believers in the Eastern dispersion, that is, in the area around Babylon. It is quite possible that this is true, although the fact that it is in Greek rather than Aramaic may raise some doubts. Certainly it was written to an area in which some of the Jews were merchants (4:13–17). This would fit very well into the idea of the Eastern dispersion.

However, it must be admitted that we cannot be positive as to the residence of the readers. We can be confident that they were Christian Jews. Where they lived does not affect the interpretation of the letter.

BACKGROUND

Two areas of thought greatly influenced the writer of this letter. Some information about the writer's background will help us understand what is being said.

Jewish

Regardless of the conclusions reached about the authorship and date of the letter of James, it is obvious that the writer was quite familiar with Jewish writings, especially the Wisdom Literature. The very nature of the writing itself follows the pattern of such literature, and the injunctions in the letter have their parallel in such writings.

Among the Old Testament books, Proverbs is the chief example of Wisdom Literature. The author of James was very familiar with the book of Proverbs and made use of material from it.

Wisdom Literature was quite common outside of the accepted

canon of the Old Testament. Two books of this nature were quite
well known and evidently influenced Paul. James was undoubtedly
familiar with both of them: Ecclesiasticus (the Wisdom of Jesus,
Son of Sirach) and the Wisdom of Solomon. There are many
places where statements in James are paralleled in these writings.
No effort has been made in this study to show these parallels.
Due to the relative unfamiliarity of these books, rather long quotations would be necessary to show the parallels. However, there
can be little doubt that material in these books was familiar to
James and was in the background of his thought.

Teachings of Jesus

Of considerably more interest to us is the very close parallel
between material in James and the teachings of Jesus, particularly
the Sermon on the Mount. Attempts are made throughout this
study to show these parallels. Undoubtedly the thoughtful reader
will discover others that are not noted. Writers have pointed out
that there are more verbal reminiscences of the teachings of
Jesus in this letter than in all the rest of the New Testament
epistles combined.

The author did not quote any statement of Jesus exactly. (It
is well to remember that if the suggested date for this letter is
correct, none of our present Gospels were yet available in written
form.) Instead, James made allusions to Jesus' teachings, putting
the statements in his own words. This seems to indicate a man
who was very much at home among these teachings. It may well
point to someone with long and intimate acquaintance with
Jesus, someone who had heard him speak time after time. Not
only had he heard him, but he had made Jesus' teachings his own.
This enabled him to make application of them to his own life
and his ministry in behalf of others.

Either this familiarity with the teachings of Jesus was firsthand
or we have, as some suggest, a much later writer who was depen-

dent upon the oral teachings of the church and the material contained in the Gospels. His sources differed from our Gospels in some details, or else he was careful never to quote any teaching of Jesus exactly. However, it seems more likely that the strong resemblances to the teachings of Jesus in this letter point to one who had been closely associated with him during, if not before, his earthly ministry.

A good preparation for the study of the letter of James would be a careful reading of the Sermon on the Mount (Matt. 5–7). Passages from these chapters will be called to mind by statements from James. In addition, other teachings of Jesus constitute the background for some of the teachings in James. It has been suggested that some otherwise unknown teachings of Jesus may be contained in this letter. However, there is no way we can be sure of this, since the author did not specify when he was making direct reference to the teachings of Jesus.

Much has been written concerning the relationship of this letter to other writings of the New Testament, especially Paul and 1 Peter. It is impossible in this brief study to enter into detailed discussion of this relationship. It has already been suggested that there appears to be no literary relationship between James and any other book of the New Testament. It is likely that this letter was written earlier than any of the writings of Paul and Peter. The fact of similarity of material simply shows that James was not in isolation from the rest of the New Testament world. His concerns were much the same as the concerns of others. They had a significance that was not limited by race and nationality or even geographical location. And we find today that their significance has not been lessened by the passage of centuries of time and the establishment of a new culture.

There are also a number of similarities between the letter of James and the letter from the Jerusalem church (Acts 15:23–29) and the speech of James at the Jerusalem conference (Acts 15:

14–21). These are "delicate similarities of thought and style too subtle for mere imitation or copying."[2] The letter from the Jerusalem church is commonly considered to be the work of James.

CHARACTERISTICS OF THE LETTER

This epistle is representative of Wisdom Literature. For the most part, it is a series of loosely connected paragraphs emphasizing various aspects of the practicality of the Christian faith. A casual reading of the letter of James may give the impression that there is no connection at all between some of the paragraphs. But, as this study proceeds, it will be seen that usually there is a connection. Sometimes the link will be repetition of some key word in the separate paragraphs.

James wrote to individuals who were already believers. Therefore, some of the basic doctrines of the Christian faith are not expressed in this letter. The way of salvation is never clearly set forth, but these were accepted facts of the Christian faith. There was no need to make them explicit in this writing.

Some have insisted, since basic Christian doctrines are so far in the background, that this is nothing more than a Jewish writing which has been "baptized into Christianity" by the inclusion of the name of Christ in isolated instances. This seems to be an unfair description of the writing and its author. To be sure, he was not interested in theological aspects to the same extent which we find in Paul or even in Peter. His interest lay in the practical outworking of the faith, and it is at this point that he put his emphasis. This is a common trait in Wisdom Literature.

The writing has few of the characteristics of a letter. The opening greeting is brief and is in the form of the customary Greek letter rather than the common Christian greeting of grace and peace. There is no expression of thanksgiving for the readers or

---

[2] A. T. Robertson, STUDIES IN THE EPISTLE OF JAMES (Nashville: Broadman Press, n.d.), p. 2.

of prayer for them. And the letter ends abruptly without any closing benediction.

The letter was written with a tone of authority. The author did not merely suggest, he commanded. "It is characteristic of the austere tone of the Epistle that it, alone of the Epistles in the New Testament, contains no attempt to conciliate the favour of the readers by direct words of praise. In it we hear the bracing call of duty uttered by one who speaks with earnest sympathy indeed and without a particle of Pharisaic assumption, but who feels that he has the right to speak and expects to be obeyed." [3] This note of authority is felt throughout the letter. It is consistent with the suggestion that the author was the brother of Jesus, the head of the Jerusalem church. James "is a preacher who speaks like a prophet . . . in language which for forcibleness is without parallel in early Christian literature, excepting the discourses of Jesus." [4]

PURPOSE

There is nothing in this letter to indicate the occasion which brought it forth. If there was some urgent crisis which led James to sit down and pen these words, we know nothing about it.

However, the purpose James had in mind is quite clear. *He wrote in an effort to convince those Jews who had become believers in Christ that their manner of life must be consistent with their claim of faith.* Not all the church members were living up to their profession. James wrote in the hope of drawing these back to the basic significance of their faith. In other words, he was concerned with moral and ethical irregularities in the lives of his readers. He challenged them to so live that their faith would be shown by their works (2:14–26). Only then could their claim to faith be justified.

---

[3] Joseph B. Mayor, THE EPISTLE OF ST. JAMES (Grand Rapids: Zondervan Publishing House, 1952), p. 133.

[4] Theodor Zahn, INTRODUCTION TO THE NEW TESTAMENT, trans. John Moore Trout et al (Grand Rapids: Kregel Publications, 1953), I, 111.

OPENING GREETING (1:1)

We have already seen that the author named himself James without any other identifying characteristics. This would indicate that he was a well-known man and that his readers could be expected to recognize him by his name. His prominence was such that they would respect his authority.

He called himself "a slave of God and of the Lord Jesus Christ." This term associates Jesus with God on a very high plane of equality.

The author was a "slave." This was a common title used by New Testament writers (Rom. 1:1; 2 Peter 1:1; Jude 1). It stressed the idea of being a worshiper. It also showed the complete surrender involved and the absolute dependence upon God. In a very real sense, every Christian is a slave of God and of the Lord Jesus Christ.

The use of the term "Lord" is also important. Jesus is more than mere man. He is Lord, Master of the individual believer. The writer of James held him in the highest possible esteem, as high as did any other writer of the New Testament.

The letter was addressed to the "twelve tribes who are in the Diaspora." These were probably Jewish Christians who lived in the dispersion in the general area of Babylon. However, it must be admitted that this is a disputed fact among New Testament scholars.

A single word is used to open the letter: "Greeting." This was the common greeting in secular Greek correspondence (note the letter from Claudius Lysias, the Roman tribune, to the governor Felix in Acts 23:26, and the letter from the Jerusalem church in Acts 15:23). The word means to be joyful. Thus, there is a connection between this greeting and the opening paragraph of the letter. It is, therefore, appropriate that the writer immediately turned to what manner of life a Christian ought to live.

2.
Trials
and
Blessings
in the
Christian
Life

Illustrative of James's forthright method is the way in which he quickly dispenses with formalities. Only twenty words in verse 1, and then he got right down to what he had to say. Compare this with most of Paul's more lengthy greetings. Read the opening verses of Ephesians, Philippians, and Colossians for instance. Paul's letters were filled with personal references and prayers of thanksgiving and petition on behalf of the readers. We do not find any of these in James's letter. Instead, he simply greeted his readers and immediately launched into the practical instructions that were his major concern.

FACING TRIALS (1:2—4)

One of the constantly recurring problems in the experience of every Christian is that of facing the difficulties that come almost daily in life. Repeatedly we ask: Why did this happen to me? And sometimes in our more depressed moments we may feel that we are receiving far worse treatment than anyone else in the world. One is reminded of the age-old question of why the unrighteous prosper and the righteous suffer. On the surface, this often does seem to be the case.

The problem of why the righteous suffer is not new. It is one that has plagued man since creation. One of the most interesting approaches to it is found in the Old Testament book of Job. He and his friends faced the question of why Job was suffering as he was. Job's answer differed from that of his friends, but they were wrestling with the same problem. And because in our day we continue to struggle with the problems of suffering, the words of James are appropriate for us.

As he began his writing, James addressed his readers as brothers. This was more than a polite or routine gesture. It showed his sympathy and concern for them. It expressed his love. And even more, it indicated his recognition of the religious ties which bound writer and reader together. He did not boast that he was the brother of Jesus, but he gladly and proudly claimed to be brother of those to whom he wrote.

In the opening verses of his letter, James was apparently concerned with two aspects of the Christian life. In verses 2 and 12 he referred to the Christian experience of suffering by using a noun which may be translated temptations or trial. In verses 13–14, he used the verb which is built upon the same root. Some translations make no distinction between the two words, translating both of them "temptation" (KJV). However, it is probably more correct to understand the noun to mean trials coming from without and the verb to mean temptations coming from within. (See RSV and almost all modern translations, along with many commentaries.) This is the position adopted in this study of what James had to say on the subject.

Attitudes Toward Trials

The way a person reacts to difficulty is a good indication of the depth of his spiritual maturity and faith. Perhaps you have observed an individual whose confidence in God was shattered by some unexpected tragedy. This is contrary to James's recommendation. He admonished the Christian to rejoice when trials come, knowing that such trials are an unavoidable part of life. No person can live long without some problems and difficulties. But instead of these being occasions of rebellion against God, they should be considered a cause of joy. James said it more forcibly. He said, "Consider it all joy." He did not mean that we should invite trouble. Neither did he mean that we are to have the "grin and bear it" attitude. We must not indulge ourselves in a "we will make the best of a bad situation" passivism. Instead, trials are to be received with a spirit of genuine rejoicing because we know the results God can bring out of suffering.

It is well at this point to remember the opening salutation and the first paragraph of the letter. The greeting in verse 1 can be expressed, "Rejoice," or "Joy to you." This greeting does not assume that all is good and pleasant. James's use of the greeting reminds us that such joy can come even in the face of affliction.

Such a suggestion may sound strange to us. Many of us have been reared to believe that we should avoid all that is unpleasant and painful, that nothing unpleasant can be helpful. But is this not one of the places where the ideas of our age are contrary to what God says? God has not promised his people that their way would always be painless and pleasant. Jesus pointed out more than once that the way of discipleship would not be easy (Matt. 5:10–12; Mark 8:34–37; 10:29–30; Luke 9:57–62).

In the days before Jesus came, people believed that trials were simply to be endured. To rejoice in trial is a New Testament idea. We who believe in Christ can look at trials from a different standpoint than does the rest of the world. For we are disciples of one who overcame death and the cross. He has shown us how to be victorious even in death. Therefore, we know that God can bring good out of even the most difficult situation. We can rejoice in this knowledge when trials come.

James did not specify the nature of these trials. Frequently it has been assumed that they were primarily religious persecutions, perhaps on the part of the government or the general populus. However, our contemporary interpretation must not limit trials to religious persecution. We do not at the moment feel the danger of such pressure. Neither did James limit his statement to one kind of trial. He spoke of "many-colored trials"; that is, all kinds of trials regardless of the source. What he said is applicable regardless of the cause of the trials. Trials may come through persecution. They may derive from the social and economic context in which we live. They may be the direct result of someone's sin. Regardless of their cause, we are to rejoice in the trials that come. This is not easy. "It is only possible when we come to think of righteousness as being infinitely more precious than comfort, happiness, or peace; when we come to see that the great thing for us in this life is not to enjoy ease and prosperity, to get rich, to rise in the world, but to become better men." [1]

James did not say that these trials come from God. The most that can be said is that God permits them to come upon his people.

Results of Trials

A Christian can rejoice in trial because he knows what can result when trial is successfully overcome. This knowledge comes from viewing the experience of others and hearing their testimony. But even more convincing is the confidence we gain when we face trial and emerge victorious. For "the proving of your faith pro-

---

[1] R. W. Dale, THE EPISTLE OF JAMES (New York: George H. Doran Company, n.d.), p. 10.

duces endurance." Here is the end toward which trial is directed. God uses these experiences to produce strength and endurance.

The idea of testing may emphasize the result of the experience more than the process. James wrote of the proven quality of faith. Faith is shown most clearly in difficulty, when things do not go right and all is not pleasant. The result of trial is that we learn how to endure. But endurance, in contrast with a common understanding of patience (KJV), is not a passive quality. Enduring does not mean that we simply put up with things because there is nothing that we can do about them. It does not mean that we are necessarily satisfied with conditions. But it indicates that we develop the strength of character that enables us, with the help of God, to be consistently and positively Christian in our approach to life. "Steadfastness" is the word used in some translations. Endurance is active; it is aggressive; it is dynamic. It enables us to accept things as they are and allows God to use them for good.

It is well to note the reference to faith at this point, since there are some readers who feel that James had a very low regard for this vital aspect of the Christian life. (This problem will be dealt with in more detail in chap. 3.) James implied that faith is at the center of the Christian experience, for it is faith that is tested in trials. It is faith that is proven by the overcoming of trial. Without faith, man is not related to God, in which case there is no quality to be proven.

Yet even endurance is not the goal of the testing process. Endurance has a further consequence. It is but a way station on the journey to the final goal: "that you may be complete and whole, lacking in nothing." Two dangers must be avoided here. We must not consider this goal of wholeness so lofty and unattainable that there is no point in striving toward it. If we adopt such an attitude, life can be lived on a low level with a clear conscience. We must also avoid the other extreme: the false assumption that perfection or completion has been attained in the conversion experi-

ence or some later experience, that because sin has been forgiven,
the individual has arrived at a point where sin is impossible. A
person holding such an idea has no strong demands of morality
made upon him. He feels free to live without any moral restraint.

Both of these ideas are contrary to God's revelation. We simply
do not become perfect at conversion. The growth toward this
goal is long and painful, and none of us will reach it in this
earthly life. Though perfection is beyond our ability to attain,
we dare not forget that it is the goal which Jesus set for us (Matt.
5:48). A lesser goal than that set by our Lord fails to call out
our best in discipleship.

The term translated complete ("perfect," KJV) means mature
or full grown. "The perfect are those who attain to the *end* for
which they were created." [2] This is always the object of life. The
goal of the growing child is physical, mental, and emotional
maturity. The goal of the growing Christian must be spiritual maturity. This can come only through the testing experiences of
life. Such experiences may be unpleasant, but the achievement of
maturity makes them worthwhile. However, James did not encourage the martyr complex. These trials are not to be sought after.
On the other hand, when trials come, they can be accepted in a new
spirit because of what God can do through them.

The word translated whole ("entire," KJV) has an Old Testament background. It was used to refer to the animal that was
sound and acceptable to God for sacrifice. James would have us
understand that trials lead to the development of spiritual and
moral soundness in order that the individual may be acceptable to
God. In this process, all parts of one's personality become complete and whole. Thus, life becomes a unity through the overcoming of trial.

The world of 1970 poses what well may be an unprecedented

---

[2] Alexander Ross, COMMENTARY ON THE EPISTLES OF JAMES AND JOHN
(Grand Rapids: William B. Eerdmans Publishing Company, 1954), p. 27.

array of problems for the believer. As we face these problems, we must do so, not limited by our own strength and understanding, but seeing things in the light of the experience of Jesus himself: "Looking to Jesus the pioneer and perfecter of our faith, who for the joy that was set before him endured the cross, despising the shame, and is seated at the right hand of the throne of God" (Heb. 12:2, RSV). The same joy can be ours, even in the face of trial. And to a large extent, the effectiveness of our Christian witness will be determined by the way the world sees us react to difficulties. Trials will come! James said that we are to rejoice in them because the greatness of their result far surpasses the discomfort they bring. (See 2 Cor. 4:17–18.)

THE GIFT OF WISDOM (1:5–8)

It may seem there is little connection between verses 5–8 and the preceding paragraph. But again James made his connection by the use of a single word. In verse 4 he wrote that the complete man lacks in nothing. Of course, no one could make such a claim of completeness, Therefore, he said, "If anyone among you lacks wisdom." Perhaps if we had been writing, we would have listed other things which were lacking before we thought of wisdom. But James saw that the road to maturity and holiness requires wisdom. Where do we get this wisdom?

The Source

We are so accustomed to equating wisdom with knowledge that it is difficult for us to understand that wisdom is not a human attainment. In this generation, great emphasis is put upon the accumulation of knowledge. It has been said that the total sum of knowledge doubles every five years, and this figure is changing rapidly. Students spend endless hours trying to acquire as much information as possible. But this is not the wisdom of which James spoke. Wisdom is not something gained from books, not even from other people. It is something which comes only as a gift from the Bible alone. It is not something acquired by conversation with God. "With James wisdom is the right use of one's opportunities in holy living. It is living like Christ in accord with the will of God." [3]

This understanding of wisdom is not unique with James. He was familiar with the book of Proverbs in the Old Testament where wisdom is exalted to a lofty degree (chaps. 8–9). James may also have been familiar with two noncanonical Jewish books of wisdom, Ecclesiasticus and the Wisdom of Solomon. In both of these books the same idea is presented—that wisdom comes from God. Of course, Solomon is the best-known example of a man with wisdom. He asked wisdom of God, and it was given to him (1 Kings 3:3–14). James was certain that any believer can ask God for wisdom and be confident that he will receive it.

Not only does God give wisdom, but he gives it "generously and without reproaching." Actually, James said God gives simply, a word which frequently, in the New Testament, carries the idea of generosity. God's gift of wisdom is generous. He does not give this gift reproachfully. And it is an unconditional gift. It is not something which is earned or bartered for. God simply gives it upon request. This causes one to recall Jesus' teaching on prayer. He encouraged his followers simply to ask of God with the confidence that he would give what was requested (Luke 11:9–13).

The Channel

James reminded his readers that the request for wisdom must be made in faith. "Faith" in our contemporary language does not carry the impact that its Greek equivalent means. The word "faith" has been misused. However, if we are to understand the New Testament, we must allow the words to convey what the writer meant. When James used the word "faith," he meant, as did Jesus

---

[3] Robertson, op. cit., p. 41.

and Paul, that *faith is trust in God.* That is, faith is a full commitment of self to God and what God wants done. Thus, the meaning is far deeper than mere belief in a dogma or acceptance of a doctrinal position.

We face the danger of assuming that if someone will subscribe to a creed or a statement of principles, he is a man of faith. In reality, it is entirely possible for someone to give his pledge to a statement of principles and still have no vital relationship with God. While it is important to be biblically correct in one's doctrine, it is even more essential that a person have the type of faith of which the New Testament speaks—complete trust in the person, the wisdom, the power, and the mercy of God. This is the kind of faith which brings wisdom in answer to prayer. If we are troubled by prayers which seemingly are unanswered, we need to take stock to see if we have asked in full trust and commitment.

The contrast to such faith is doubt. The word used here by James means double-minded. Such a person is constantly in the position of not knowing whether or not really to trust God. At one moment he wants to trust him, but at the next he has no confidence in God and depends upon himself. James described him as "a surging of the sea, wind tossed and billowing." The picture is of one who is constantly shifting, one who is unstable and undependable. When we approach God with an attitude such as this, we have no right to expect to receive anything from him.

ATTITUDE TOWARD MATERIAL THINGS (1:9-11)

James seemed to realize that a person's attitude toward material things is a good index of his spiritual condition. He also realized that this is one area of life where most believers have problems. How easy it is to get caught up in the rat race of life and lose sight of things of God that matter. Each of us would have to admit to the appeal of materialism in today's culture. The Christian must be careful to avoid this pitfall.

In this brief paragraph (vv. 9–11) is the first contrast between the poor and rich. In some instances the rich are singled out for severe criticism from James. The rich are sometimes bitterly opposed in this letter, probably because they oppress the believers. However, in verses 9–11, James seems to have been referring to Christians who are rich. James's point here is that in the Christian brotherhood riches do not count. He discussed the proper attitude toward material things regardless of whether one is rich or poor. A poor man who longs for material things may be as guilty of greed as the rich man.

By the Humble

Again we see that by the use of a single word or idea James linked his new material to what had been said previously. In this instance (v. 9), the word "boast" picks up the idea of "all joy" in verse 2. It means to rejoice or have joy or boast in one's condition. So, we are called back to the sense of joy that introduced the letter.

Concerning what is the poor or lowly man to boast? Certainly he will not brag about his poverty. But since he is a believer, he can boast, or find joy, because he has been exalted spiritually (Matt. 5:3). Such a man is the exact opposite of the double-minded man of the previous paragraph. This lowly brother is stable and settled in his allegiance to God in Jesus Christ. He can take joy in Christ because in him all men are equal.

God shows no partiality (Acts 10:34). There must be no class distinctions in the Christian community. While the lowly man may be debased in his economic or social position, within the church fellowship he has his dignity restored because he has been accepted by Christ. He is a person. Jesus said, "Whoever humbles himself will be exalted" (Matt. 23:12). Such a man is not poor or lowly in God's sight. He can boast of his worth as a person in the sight of God and for what he has received from God.

In a day when material wealth is often the entire focus of attention, it is well to realize that degree of economic success is never a safe measure of a person's true worth or wealth. True riches are to be found in the areas of grace, love, and righteousness. The humble and lowly possess these, and such qualities are often missed by the rich and the proud. In a society geared to measuring by material standards, the emphasis of James is a much-needed one.

By the Rich

Just as the poor man boasts in his exaltation, so the rich man should boast "in his being made low." Two questions emerge here. First, is this a Christian rich man to whom reference is made? Elsewhere in this writing the references to the rich seem to indicate that they are unbelievers. They oppress the Christians and blaspheme the name of Christ (2:6–7). They are proud and boast in their arrogance (4:16). They are the ones who have cheated and condemned (5:1–6). While this is the general appraisal of the rich throughout the letter, in this particular instance there is no condemnation of the rich as a group. Instead, the rich man seems to be considered from the same viewpoint as the poor man— he is a Christian brother.

Another question to consider: What does it mean for such a rich man to be made low? This expression may have only a figurative significance and refer to the self-surrender which is involved in becoming a Christian. On the other hand, many commentators feel that James may have been referring to instances when the rich man meets trials which result in the loss of much of his riches. This could result from his becoming a Christian since he could now face opposition from those with whom he formerly associated in the business world. Or, it may be that he would have less riches because his business practices were no longer so selfish and corrupt. Whatever the case, it is clear that

James's main concern was the new attitude of the individual toward things. No longer is his confidence to be found in his possessions. These possessions are seen in their true light, and his confidence is now in his Lord (Matt. 6:19–21). He is truly humbled and in this he can honestly boast. Zacchaeus illustrates the required change of attitude to which James pointed (Luke 19:1–10).

James saw clearly the true nature of riches. They are not permanent; they are easily lost; and it is dangerous to trust in them. The image he painted must have been one which was thoroughly familiar to any person who had spent any time in Palestine. The loveliest flower could be wilted and destroyed in a brief time by the burning wind from the desert. This extremely hot wind could arise in a short time and scorch any plant in its path. It was feared by the farmer of Palestine. Even the finest crop could not withstand its fury.

Such are the trials which come upon the one who trusts in riches. He will "waste away in the midst of his goings." This could be the case of the rich merchant. Even while he is busily engaged in his trade, he will discover that his riches have vanished. What desolation comes in such a life. All that matters has vanished; nothing worthwhile remains. The rich Christian is insured against such a fate, for he no longer trusts in his perishable riches. Even if his riches should perish, the Christian has another foundation. His life has been built upon the rock, not on the shifting sand (Matt. 7:24–27). His boast is in the Lord, not in himself or his possessions.

THE REWARD FOR ENDURANCE (1:12)

With the reference to trial in verse 12, James returned to one strand of the thought of verses 2–4. He seems to have realized that there would be times when the Christian would wonder if the victory would be worth the cost. The desire to avoid unpleasantness is an ever-present reality in life. So James presented further encouragement to those who would face trials.

Verse 12 is reminiscent of Jesus. He used the expression "blessed" a number of times (Matt. 5:3–11). James used it here to speak of the reward that comes to the one who endures trial. "Blessed is the man who endures trial." But what does the word "blessed" mean? Some have suggested that it means to be happy; others suggest that it means to be congratulated—congratulations because of the reward which is promised the man who endures trial.

The trial referred to here is the same type spoken of earlier. It is one which comes from without, not from within. The trial shows that which is pure and unadulterated. The one who is tested and emerges victorious is one whose faith is strong and secure. Such a person deserves to be congratulated.

The reward which is received is "the crown, which is life, which God promised to those who love him." These words call to mind the words to the church at Smyrna: "Become faithful unto death, and I will give to you the crown, which is life" (Rev. 2:10). It has been suggested that this promise of a crown of life comes from an unrecorded saying of Jesus when he promised life to those who love him. We cannot be sure he made such a statement, but it would be in keeping with other teachings of Jesus.

But what kind of life is referred to here? Is the reference only to physical life? Or, is life used in the fuller sense of eternal, spiritual life? In all probability the reference is to eternal life. Jesus promised true life, eternal life, to the one who really loves him. To these he gives "the crown, which is life." The picture may be drawn from the crown or wreath placed upon the head of the victor in the race. However, such a crown, though a coveted honor, does not last long. The one who loves Jesus receives an imperishable crown. "Everyone who contends for a prize exercises self-control in all things. They, then, do it in order that they may receive a perishable crown, but we to receive an imperishable" (1 Cor. 9:25).

WARNING AGAINST TEMPTATION (1:13–15)

Some commentators feel that James was referring to temptation in verse 12. Certainly it is but a short step from speaking of outward trial to speaking of inward temptation. However, the transition from one to the other more likely comes in verse 13. It is clear that in this brief paragraph (vv. 13–15) James wrote about the terrible reality of temptation, whether it comes as the direct result of trial or from some other cause.

The Source of Temptation

It is true of human nature that we never like to admit our responsibility for failure or error. It eases our consciences if we can blame a failure or a sin on someone else. So it is quite popular to say our offenses are due to heredity—we are what we are because of the genes we have inherited from our parents. Thus, the blame ultimately goes back to them, and the punishment rightfully belongs to them instead of to us. This is much like the Hebrews' concept of visiting the sins of the parent upon the third and fourth generation (Ex. 34:6–7), a concept which was condemned by the later prophets (Jer. 31:29–30; Ezek. 18:1–4).

Or, we may be inclined to place all blame for our faults upon our environment: How can we be expected to behave any better with evil all about us? We are likely to reason that our surroundings are what lead us to sin; therefore, the blame cannot be put upon us alone. Or it may be that we will put the blame upon Satan as Eve did when she said: "The serpent beguiled me, and I did eat" (Gen. 3:13, KJV). Certainly the attitude of Adam is common. It was not his fault, he pointed out. "The woman whom thou gavest to be with me, she gave me of the tree, and I did eat" (Gen. 3:12, KJV). All of these are attempts to transfer the blame elsewhere. And in Adam's reply can be found the attempt to put the blame upon God himself. God gave the woman to Adam. Therefore, since she led him into sin, Adam inferred that God was at least partly responsible.

This same attitude toward God is reflected in the all-too-frequent attempt to blame God for what we are and how we are made. God made man, we are prone to reason; therefore, God must be responsible for man's weaknesses and failures. God permits all things to happen. God controls his creation. It follows, we are likely to rationalize, that nothing happens without his permitting it to do so. Therefore, he is responsible for temptation and ultimately the sin which results from it. This is the line of reasoning James knew was being used by some of his readers.

James refused to accept such an idea. He pointed out that temptation comes from within the individual and not from anything outside. This explains why one thing may be a temptation to one man and not to another. One man walks down the street and undergoes an almost unbearable temptation to enter the liquor store or bar. For a second man, this is not temptation at all. What makes the difference? It is not the outward situation but the inward condition. So, man must not place the blame for temptation on God. For "God is untempted by evil, and he himself tempts no one." "No one can tempt another to evil unless he himself has some experience [and, it is implied, enjoyment] in yielding to temptation." [4] The idea that God tempts men is a ridiculous idea indeed. Instead of being holy, righteous, merciful, and gracious, he would be like the gods of the pagans before whom one had to cringe in terror and dread because these gods were fickle and temperamental. This is not the kind of God revealed in the Bible. This is not the kind of God revealed in his Son, Jesus Christ.

---

[4] James Moffatt, THE GENERAL EPISTLES (New York: Harper-Row, n.d.), p. 18.

It is God who gives the power to overcome temptation. He is the one to whom we are encouraged to pray: "Do not lead us into temptation, but deliver us from the evil one" (Matt. 6:13).

In all honesty, we must admit that temptation comes from within. Not only does it come from within, it is the result of our own evil desire. James used very vivid language to describe the process. He wrote of being "drawn out and enticed." This is the picture of the fisherman. He dangles the bait before the fish, lures him out of his hiding place, and catches him on his hook. This is the way desire works. It lures and entices the individual until he is caught in the snare of sin. While these words were often used to depict the enticement of the harlot, there is no reason to restrict James's discussion here to sexual sin. The same process occurs with all temptation.

Temptation enters and the individual falls victim to it. How often such a process repeats itself in our lives. This admission may harm our ego, but such an awareness may help us avoid the fatal allurement of temptation. The wise person resists temptation, attempts to avoid it. It is so deadly a game that only a fool seeks it.

To be sure, desire can be good. We can want a good thing as well as an evil thing. We do not accomplish much without desiring to do so. No athlete is victorious without strong motivation. No team wins without drive. But when what we want is evil and we allow our wants to press for fulfilment until we are filled with desire for some evil thing, then we are victimized by our evil desires. We are tempted. We yield and this is sin. This is the process which James had reference to in this passage. Desire is frequently translated "lust." While sexual sin is only one aspect of sinful desire, it may have suggested the image in verse 16.

The Results of Yielding

James did not suggest that the temptation itself is sin. Even Jesus was tempted (Luke 4:1–13; Heb. 4:15). It is yielding to temptation that brings tragic consequences. This is why temptation is so dangerous and should never be sought, for one never knows when he may weaken and yield. God promises the necessary strength to overcome temptation, but too often we do not make use of this strength; and the result is sin.

James used the image of birth and growth to show the results of yielding to temptation. The giving in to desire or lust James likened to conception. And that which is born from this conception is sin. "The mere fact of our being tempted does not involve in itself anything sinful. It is when the desire of man goes out to meet and embrace the forbidden thing and an unholy marriage takes place between these two, that sin is born." [5] There is no effort made to distinguish between various types of sin. Our distinctives between greater and lesser sins are not scriptural.

Sin is born! It develops and, when it becomes full grown, it brings forth death. There is much discussion as to what is meant in the Scriptures when it is said that death is the result of sin. (Paul likewise said, "The wages of sin is death," Rom. 6:23.) Clearly, spiritual death is the result of sin; it separates the individual from God. Since this death is brought about by sin, sin must be avoided by the one who would live close to God and please him.

While desire may seem so innocent and yielding to it so pleasant, we need to remember the fatal results of yielding to temptation. How utterly foolish it is to place ourselves in situations where temptation is certain to come! God cannot tolerate sin in the lives of his people; therefore, sin must be punished. While we know that Christ died for our sins, we need to remember Paul's words of warning: "Shall we abide in sin so that grace may abound? Certainly not! How shall we who died to sin live any longer in it?" (Rom. 6:1-2).

---

[5] Ross, *op. cit.*, p. 34.

BLESSINGS FROM GOD (1:16–18)

In verse 16, James seems to be alluding to false teachings. He knew that God could not tempt anyone. God gives only that which is good and helpful. Perhaps James had reference to those who were teaching that God is the source of all things, including evil. Men forget that God has never promised absolute safety in a world in which there is evil and sin. He has never promised to protect people from their own sin or the sins of others. So the caution is necessary: "Stop being deceived." This may indicate that some dangerous teachings about temptation and sin were actually making inroads among the believers.

Gifts

Instead of tempting men to sin, God gives good gifts. "All good giving and every perfect gift is from above." Two ideas are contained in this statement: Whatever good may come in life comes from God, and whatever God gives is good. Sincere study of the Bible will show this to be true. Serious thought about our own experience should confirm it. Throughout the Bible God is pictured as the giver of good. This was true in the experiences of Adam and Eve (Gen. 2:15–25). It was true in the selection of Abraham to be the father of a new race to serve as a blessing to the other peoples of the world (Gen. 12:1–3). It was true in his raising up a deliverer in the person of Moses (Ex. 3:1–12). Supremely, it was shown to be true in the gift of God's Son for the redemption of man. Can you think of any good thing that has come in your life which has not come either as a direct or indirect result of God's giving?

The realization of God's goodness helps us to put life in a better perspective. How easy it is in an age of compartmentalization to push God off to one side. Man has learned to do almost everything worthwhile himself. He can send men and machinery to the moon and the planets. He can use scientific know-how to test and analyze soil on those far-off bodies. Man has the ability to create a better society, although he has not learned how to control himself enough to make the creation a reality. He has learned how to control and conquer many of the worst diseases. He can increasingly prolong life. As this is being written, the first seemingly successful heart transplants have taken place. Some scientists even believe that man is on the verge of creating life in the test tube. Does man need God any longer? Yes, he needs him perhaps more than any age of man has needed God. It is true that life in the seventies is a technological wonder. But this is only because of the good gifts that keep coming from God. It is God who has guided the mind of man to all of these fantastic achievements. "All good giving and every perfect gift is from above." Man does not and cannot stand on his own. He needs a God who loves and who gives.

Faithfulness

The realization that God does not change is a second blessing which James found in his understanding of God. The good of which he has spoken comes down "from the Father of lights with whom there is no change or shadow cast by turning." James probably used the language of popular astronomy in this description of God. As can be seen by comparing various translations, there is no absolute agreement as to the details of the comparison he made. Some feel he was thinking about such things as the darkness at night when the sun is on the opposite side of the earth, or the light of the moon being shut off by the shadow of the earth. Other interpreters feel that James was referring to the different positions of the sun and the other heavenly bodies in the sky at various times. It is not necessary to know beyond question the facts of the imagery used. The truth being conveyed seems clear: While all created things, even the heavenly bodies, change, *there is absolutely no change with God.*

There is, of course, the recognition here that God is the Creator of the heavenly bodies. James did not share the idea that matter is evil and could not have been created by God. Neither did he agree with ancient (and modern) astrology that the heavenly bodies control the lives of men and nations. Such ideas were prominent in ancient days and still hold sway over the minds of many people. James saw that the stars and the planets are parts of God's creation and, as with all other parts of his creation, are subject to continual change. However, God does not change (Mal. 3:6). He is one upon whom we can absolutely depend with the assurance that our faith in him will not prove to be in vain. The author of Hebrews echoed this assurance when he said, "Jesus Christ is the same yesterday, today, and forever" (13:8).

New Birth

The final blessing of which James wrote in this passage is, to use Jesus' term, the new birth. Actually, this is the greatest of all God's blessings, the highest of his gifts, and the final outcome of his faithfulness. James suggested three significant points about this new birth.

The first is the fact that this *activity of God is purposeful.* It is done "by his own will." It is something which has always been in the purpose and plan of God. It was determined by him even before the beginning of creation. Salvation, the new birth, is not a mere accident. Neither is it brought about at the initiative of man. The New Testament is clear that all that is involved in salvation is the work of God. "For you are saved by grace through faith; and this is not from you, it is the gift of God" (Eph. 2:8). James would be in basic agreement with this statement which was written many years later.

The second suggestion is that *the new birth is accomplished by the "word of truth."* Many ideas come to mind with this expression. We are immediately reminded of the account of creation ın Genesis 1, where again and again it is said that God spoke and it came to pass. The word of God had creative power in the beginning. In a similar way, God's word continues to have life-giving power. Jesus commanded the demons to come out of the possessed, and it was done (Luke 4:31–37). The Roman army officer saw that Jesus was a man of authority and realized that Jesus only needed to speak a word and his servant would be healed (Luke 7:1–10). Jesus spoke of God's word as being truth (John 17:17). In James's day, the idea may have been enlarged to include the gospel, for it is by the preaching of the gospel that men come to saving faith in Jesus Christ. The word of truth is powerful to convert the sinner (Heb. 4:12).

The third idea which James expressed is that *believers become the firstfruits of God's creatures.* "Firstfruits" is a term often used in the Old Testament. The people brought the first of the harvest as an offering to God (Deut. 26:1–11). It signified their recognition that all things belong to God and their faith that God would bless the remainder of the harvest. Christians are such firstfruits. First-century Christians could look beyond themselves as the beginning of God's great harvest with the assurance that the completion of the harvest would come in due time. We may look at ourselves in the same way. We, too, are firstfruits. We have not yet seen the completion of the harvest. Greater days lie ahead for God's people if we realize we belong to him and commit ourselves in faith to his will.

The new birth is the greatest blessing God can give. Because we love God and men, we desire that all share the glorious blessing of this new birth, along with all the other blessings which God continues to give.

3.
Practical
Aspects
of Faith

Early in his epistle James made it clear that all that is good in life is a gift from God. And the supreme gift from God is the new life we have through Jesus Christ. Because every blessing from God involves a responsibility, we must ask, What does God expect from us to whom he has so generously given all things?

WORKING THE RIGHTEOUSNESS OF GOD (1:19–21)

God expects and demands righteousness in his people. Since he himself is holy and without sin, he cannot tolerate sin in the lives of his children. When we are saved, we receive righteousness which brings, as Paul used the term, acceptance by God. We have taken on the nature of God and can be called children of God. Though we have been accepted by God, our righteousness is imperfect. With God's help we strive to root out the imperfections. James gave certain suggestions that are helpful in our effort to achieve God's standard of righteousness.

Before he launched into these suggestions, James gave an imperative: "Know this." ("Wherefore" in the KJV followed by recent translators.) This expression suggests that what follows is of importance and should be heeded. The readers should be prepared to act on the basis of their knowledge.

Once more the readers were addressed as brothers, with the word "beloved" added. This term helps to remove the harshness of what James had to say. He wanted his readers to know that he spoke in love and under the leadership of the Holy Spirit.

Avoiding Anger

Anger is the greatest weakness in the lives of many people. There are people who are plagued by what we call an uncontrollable temper. Some people flare up with slight provocation. Others are generally even tempered but on occasion will become very angry. Only a few persons have arrived at the point where they keep their temper under complete control. It is easy to see the evil of anger in the lives of others, but most of us are tempted to justify our anger by referring to it as righteous indignation.

In an effort to get his readers to be aware of their problem and to seek to overcome it, James encouraged them to be swift or quick to hear and slow to speak. These are difficult traits to achieve. Most of us are quite willing to give advice whether it is desired or not. It is hard to learn to be a good listener. We have trouble understanding that when people come to us for help, the thing they want most is a sympathetic ear. What a comfort it is to have someone to whom we can tell our burdens and troubles, knowing that they will listen patiently, prayerfully, and sympathetically. Sometimes advice is helpful; more frequently good listening is the essential. Certainly we cannot even give needed advice if we have not first listened.

In a frighteningly depersonalized society, most of us have developed the capability of tuning people out. We may sit and appear to listen, but we hear almost nothing of what is being said. Any Christian who desires to help those in need must develop the ability to be "quick to hear."

Next James gave a warning against speaking too quickly. This trait is brother to that of being a poor listener. Why do we feel that we must say something in every situation? Is it not possible that at times a clasp of the hand, a pat on the back, or a smile may speak more meaningfully to the need of a person than a thousand words?

Of course, our problem may not be that we speak too quickly. Instead, we may be prone to leave the most important things unsaid. We have no difficulty talking about fashions, weather, politics, or the affairs of the world. But we become timid and hesitant whenever the opportunity comes to bear witness of what God has done for us and desires to do for others. Certainly we should not be hesitant about witnessing. However, the advice of James is still of significance: Be slow to speak. Many people talk far too much.

There is a close connection between anger and speaking too quickly, for anger is most frequently expressed by the spoken word. To be sure, at times anger may express itself in action, harsh and deadly. This must be avoided at all costs. But we sin more frequently by showing our anger in our speech. Often we say things in the heat of emotion that we would never dream of saying in calmer moments, and the spoken word can never be recalled. It does its damage and this is often irreparable. No wonder James had so much to say about the control of the tongue (3:1–12).

James was not the only one who emphasized the danger of anger. Jesus warned against it in the Sermon on the Mount (Matt.

5:22). On more than one occasion, Paul warned against anger (Eph. 4:31; Col. 3:8). While there is some mention of righteous indignation or some recognition of holy anger, the Scriptures do not support the idea that we are doing God's will and purpose when we act out of uncontrolled anger.

Putting Off Wickedness

A second action necessary in accomplishing God's righteousness is to put off all evil. "Wherefore, put off all filthiness and abundance of evil and in meekness receive the implanted word which is able to save your lives." This is similar to Paul's instruction to put off the old man and to put on the new man (Eph. 4:22–24).

James stated this change of nature in a way to show that it is to be a once-for-all decision. Of course, we realize this is not an act which has removed all evil from our lives, but the removal of all evil is the goal and ultimate consequence. An individual who claims to belong to Christ yet insists that his life is not under the moral government of God does not understand the basic tenets of discipleship. The believer has become a new creation (2 Cor. 5:17), and this change is to show in his life. The evil and wicked qualities which are accumulated through the years must be disposed of as old garments are removed from the body and destroyed when they become contaminated. Consider the care taken with garments that have become radioactive. They are put aside forever. So the believer parts with his old life of sin when he becomes a follower of the Christ. All his evil must be put aside. God is not pleased with partial obedience.

"Filthiness" includes the idea of moral failure. This failure is not confined to moral areas only, but James expected his readers to be vividly aware of this aspect of filthiness. God's high standard of morality needs emphasis in the seventies also. More and more our society moves away from fixed standards of morality. There is need for renewed interest in Christian standards. However, lest we be content with simply *not* doing some things generally thought of as bad, we need to see that this "filthiness" also refers to malice. A moralist can have a vicious nature in his heart.

The second term used, "naughtiness" or "evil," denotes evil in general. James did not support the idea that some evil is all right when he used the word "superfluity" or "abundance." Instead, he meant that all evil, no matter how great or small the amount, must be removed. Only as the individual does this can he begin to approach the stature that God expects of his children.

Receiving the Implanted Word

It is not enough to put off evil. Something good must take its place (Luke 11:24–26). So James encouraged his readers to "receive in meekness the implanted word which is able to save your lives." The Word probably refers to the gospel. The individual must open up his mind and heart to allow God's Word and Spirit to enter and accomplish the wonderful and mysterious work of redemption. This word is not inherited in physical birth. It must be received. It is planted into the person. Or, to change the figure, it is grafted on. The expression had rich meaning for those with an agricultural background. Today it becomes significant for us as we read about the transplant of human organs. Such transplants save lives in a physical sense. The implanting of God's word saves life in a spiritual sense. For it is in receiving this word of faith that we find the way to a real life and that we find the way to receive forgiveness of sin.

The word must be received in meekness. This means that we must be submissive to God and have a teachable spirit. Pride must be set aside, for it is one of man's great hindrances in his approach to God. We want something of which we may boast before God. This is impossible! Salvation is God's gift to all who will receive it. Man can only accept it, not earn it.

HEARERS OR DOERS (1:22-25)

In these verses, James returned to his injunction: "Be quick to hear." But he knew that some would be satisfied with mere hearing. While it is important to listen, he knew well that more is required of the man who seeks to please God. Therefore, he contrasted two types of men: those who merely hear, and those who act as well as hear.

Those Who Hear Only

James began with the positive: "Become doers of the word." Then he put this aside until after he had more fully discussed the negative.

The picture of the hearer calls to mind the reading of the Scriptures in the Temple. James spoke of one who is content to hear and do nothing. Such a man deceives himself. It is tragic enough for a person to be deceived by others, but there is something especially pathetic about the individual who is guilty of self-deception. That is precisely what one does to himself when he hears the Word of God taught or preached, gives assent to its truth and timeliness, and all the while lives an unchanged life.

Our churches have in them those who are content to listen so long as no action is required. It does not cost anything to listen; it requires little energy and no involvement. But those who thus limit their relationship to the gospel have missed the whole point. Jesus never called anyone merely to be a listener. He challenged the fishermen: "Come after me, and I will make you to become fishers of men" (Mark 1:17). He commissioned his followers: "You will receive power when the Holy Spirit comes upon you, and you will be my witnesses" (Acts 1:8). His call was always to follow and to go, never simply to sit and to listen.

James compared the hearer to a man who takes a hurried glance in the mirror to make sure his appearance is proper but pays no attention to the details he sees there. It is a mere cursory look.

And as soon as he goes about his business, he forgets all that he saw.

Mirrors in the first century were made of polished metal and were not as clear as the ones with which we are familiar. At best, they would give only a distorted image. Thus, Paul spoke of seeing in a mirror darkly (1 Cor. 13:12). The image was always to some extent a poor representation of the person. The reflection would be like that which you would see when looking in a clear pool of water.

James said the man looked at the "face of his birth." Most interpret this to mean looking at his outward physical appearance only. This is in contrast to the individual who takes a close inward look at himself as revealed by God's Word.

The action of the individual who takes this glance is abrupt. He wastes no time. He looks and then hastens off to his daily activities. There is no delay and the impression made upon him is only too brief. He goes about his work with no more thought of his appearance.

This is a good picture of the one who hears only. The things which he hears never penetrate beneath the level of the skin. No matter what is said, nothing happens. There is no conviction of sin, no realization of wrongdoing. There is no deepening of love and no compassion for the lost. There is no encouragement to service and no pricking of the conscience because of the realization that God expects more than is being done. The life of the person is unaffected. This is the tragedy of the hearer who never responds or acts upon what he hears.

Those Who Hear and Do

The contrast of the doer with the hearer is quite pointed. The word used by James for "doer" may give the impression of bending over to get a close look (1 Peter 1:12). The doer takes a more careful look than does the hearer at how life is to be lived.

A second comparison is that the doer looks into the "perfect law of liberty," while the hearer looks only in the imperfect metal mirror. James was addressing himself to many Hebrews who had sought to live by the law, Torah. They looked upon the Torah—a term meaning teaching, direction, revelation—as a fundamental part of their covenant relationship with God. The entire Torah was read each year as a part of their worship. Though the Jews loved the law and delighted in it, their keeping of it was hindered by their human imperfection. So James spoke of a "perfect law of liberty." It is "perfect" because it was made complete by Christ. It is the "law of liberty" because it can be observed by men who are free in Christ.

It is significant that the man looks into the law. No doubt the law of which James wrote can probably be most adequately referred to as the gospel. The hearer looks at the law carefully. He searches it to find its truths for himself. It is a law which can and does reveal man to himself. He sees himself as he really is and as God sees him. He sees his sin, he repents, and he turns to God.

James wrote of a law which a man chooses to accept and follow. It is not forced on him. But he considers it and selects it as his own. Under this law of liberty man finds the only true freedom there is. Jesus had said, "You will know the truth and the truth will set you free" (John 8:32). There is no real liberty apart from Christ. Man is enslaved to sin and there is no power to release him from that slavery other than that which he receives from Christ. "The Christian gospel is a law of liberty because it creates in the hearts of those who perfectly receive it the disposition and the power to obey it." [1]

James also contrasted the forgetful hearer and the doer who remains or perseveres. The "hearer only" glances into the truth and immediately hurries off to the daily routine. The doer is so attracted by his close look at God's revelation that he remains close

---

[1] Dale, op. cit., p. 50.

to learn from it and to be guided by it. It is possible to hear God's Word and not persevere long enough in study for this Word to make its proper impact. The doer, however, perseveres in this study of the Scriptures and this leads him to become a doer of work rather than a forgetful hearer.

James placed the stress upon the positive kind of hearer, the doer of work. This man is the center of attention, and he is the one who "will be blessed in his doing." The use of the word blessed is reminiscent of the Beatitudes of the Sermon on the Mount (Matt. 5:3–11). The word is sometimes translated happy or to be congratulated. In James it may mean that the person who is active in doing what God requires will be rewarded by God. The New Testament clearly teaches that there will be reward for faithful service although it does not place the emphasis upon this as the most important motivation for service. The doer of work is the one who receives God's reward and commendation rather than the one who merely sits back and listens without acting (Matt. 7:21–27). While it is good to be quick to hear, it is also essential to act upon that which is heard.

RESTRAINT OF THE TONGUE (1:26)

Warnings concerning the use of the tongue are repeated in this letter. It has already been seen that James pinpointed the tendency to speak too quickly as one of the real problems for the Christian. This might include speaking too much and speaking without thinking. At this point in his writing he insisted that the tongue must be kept under control.

James wrote about the man who considered himself to be re-ligious. Picture the man: He gives every outward evidence of piety and devotion. He attends church services with regularity. He takes an active part in the work of his church. He reads his Bible, prays in public, and probably is a tither. In other words, he goes through all the outward forms of religion. Why, he gives every indication to the world and to his fellow church members that he is a true Christian. But look a little closer. There is one fault that goes deep, though he considers this to be minor. He cannot control his tongue. In spite of this, he thinks he is religious. And, as with the man who was merely a hearer, he is deceiving himself. Thus, James offered an illustration of the self-deception mentioned in verse 22.

It is easy for us to go through the motions of being religious without controlling our tongues. James spoke of putting a bridle on the tongue. He knew that a horse can be controlled with a bridle. The tongue, just as headstrong and capable of self-assertion as the strong-willed horse, must also be controlled. Otherwise, all religious practices can only be deception. Others may not be fooled, but the individual with the unbridled tongue is deceiving himself.

When the tongue is not controlled, all religious practice is a waste of time and energy. When we speak eloquently of the Christian virtue of patience and lose our own at the slightest provocation, our speaking is accepted as insincere. When we extol the grace of love, and speak hatefully to another, who is going to believe that we know anything about love?

Note that James did not comment on the extreme wickedness of what was said. The person was not accused of cursing or even of gossip. These might have been his faults, but James's comment was not limited to that. It was just that the tongue was not under control. If a person desires to be pleasing to God, then this fault must be overcome.

OUTWARD AND INWARD QUALITIES OF RELIGION (1:27)

After he talked of the negative aspect that makes all religious practices useless, James returned to talk of positive things. What is true religious practice? How does the person act who is a doer of the Word and not a hearer only? Assuming his tongue is under control, what else will be found in his life? James listed two characteristics—one expressed outwardly in the man's relation to other people, and the second expressed inwardly in his own personal character.

Assistance to the Needy

"Religion that is pure and undefiled before God the Father is this: to visit orphans and widows in their affliction." This advice from James is quite in keeping with the practical nature of his writing. We may talk all we wish about our relation to God, but all our talk is vain unless it shows in our relationship with other people. In other words, religious practice is more than the personal matter of a man's relationship with God. (We would often like to restrict it to that because it makes fewer demands upon us.)

Jesus emphasized the practical outworking of our faith. The parable of the good Samaritan (Luke 10:30–37) is a clear example of this. The priest and the Levite would have claimed to be religious, but they failed to minister to the man in need. The Samaritan, despised and shunned by the Jew, was the hero of the story. He showed mercy to the one in need.

Furthermore, Jesus demonstrated in his own life that concern for others is a necessary quality of religious practice. He was not afraid to associate with sinners and tax collectors, although such people were outcasts and were hated by the religious groups. Jesus was severely criticized for his association with them, but he made it clear that he came to minister to all persons in need. His response to the criticism was: "I have not come to call righteous men but sinners to repentance" (Luke 5:32). He saw men who were hungry and fed them; he saw those who were ill and healed their bodies. He was concerned for every need of man. Giving emphasis to the same matter, John wrote: "Whoever has the goods of the world and sees his brother in need and shuts off his compassion from him, how does the love of God abide in him?" (1 John 3:17).

The two categories of persons of greatest need in James's day were the orphans and widows. The number of orphans was undoubtedly in much greater proportion than it is today. There was great need among widows. There were no public agencies available to care for either group. Widows could not get employment to provide for themselves, so the only hope was that the religious community would make provision for them. The Jews had been very helpful in this area of service. Such people were considered the special concern of God (Psalm 68:5). The church at Jerusalem took care of the widows within its fellowship (Acts 6:1). Very specific instructions were laid down concerning their enrolment (1 Tim. 5:3–16). James stated that these groups were to be visited. And the word translated visit means to visit with a view of providing help (Luke 1:68; 7:16). Scholars have noted that this word can mean to look upon, care for, exercise oversight. They were to do more than "go calling"; they were to take care of those in need.

When we translate this into our own society, what areas of need open up where we may demonstrate that our religion is true? To be sure, we must never lose sight of the spiritual needs of people, but religion is always concerned to go further than this. Physical needs also claim our attention. And it should be emphasized that religion is not an "either-or" situation, *either* meeting the spiritual needs *or* caring for the physical needs of men. It is "both-and"— meeting the spiritual and the physical needs of persons.

In a day when the government has taken the initiative in most welfare programs, there is the tendency to feel that the church has no responsibility in this area. One of the reasons why welfare has become such a large area of governmental concern is our failure to meet the needs of those within our fellowship. We are doing some work in the providing of child care facilities, providing for the senior citizens, and building hospitals for the ill. This has been done as a cooperative denominational effort. But what about the local congregation and the individual Christian? We must find ways to express our religion in a practical way. We must train ourselves to be alert to human need. We must plan our church programs so that meeting needs will not require out-of-the-ordinary action. We must plan our work so that an integral part of the church life is meeting special needs of persons both inside and outside the fellowship.

How we go about meeting needs of persons will vary in different communities. We must be alert to see needs. Recently, there was the report of a family discovered starving to death on the second floor of a building. A church occupied the lower floor for its meeting place. What would James have said about the religious practice of this group? We must seek to minister to people as best we can in the name of Christ. Not to do so will make all of our fine words sound very hollow to those in desperate need.

Personal Purity

There is also an inner quality that must be cultivated by the Christian. The believer must keep himself spotless from the world. This is the inward look. It requires the realization that no matter how busy we may be in witnessing and seeking to help others, we must avoid sin in our own lives. It is easy to get so involved in *doing* that we forget the necessity of *being*. We can readily see faults in the lives of others and overlook those in our own lives (Matt. 7:3–5). We may become so busy in our institutional expressions of religion that we neglect to find time for private expressions: Bible study, prayer, and meditation. Before we are aware of it, sin begins to make inroads, our spiritual vitality dries up, and we become useless in the service of Christ and perhaps even a disgrace to his name. No person is immune to this danger. We need to be aware of it in order that we may keep ourselves without stain.

In this verse the world is thought of as that which is in opposition to God. It may be evil in and of itself. There are many
things in the world of which this is true. Christians must avoid
these obvious evils. Other things in the world may not be sinful
in themselves, but under certain circumstances they can be in
opposition to God and his work. It is at the point of recognizing
these that Christians need wisdom from God (James 1:5). Anything which is contrary to God's will and purpose at a given
moment must be avoided. Anything which would call us from
our loyalty to God, anything which would put self back at the
center of life, anything which would harm others—these things
are "of the world" and bring stain and spot upon the life of the
believer.

James provided us with a healthy view of life. He was not one-
sided. He warned Christians against giving complete attention to
self. At the same time, he did not indicate that one must forget
self in his concern with service to others. He recognized that the
two go hand in hand. There is need for us today to look carefully at ourselves to see if we are maintaining this proper balance.
"Pure and undefiled" religious practice looks outward in practical
assistance to others in need, and it looks inward to keeping the life
of the believer pure and wholesome.

THE EVILS OF PARTIALITY (2:1–7)

There are many ways in which our faith may be made meaningless so far as our relation with others is concerned. One of these
is respect of persons or the showing of partiality. This particular
sin involves every one of us because there are many aspects of it.
We are tempted to think of it in only one way in our country—
in the matter of race. While this aspect is important, we must not
limit respect of persons to race conflicts alone. In fact, the example
which James used is one where we are often blind and do not
see our own guilt.

He pictured two men coming into the Christian meeting. One of them was rich and the other was poor. This was obvious from the way in which they were dressed. One wore fine clothing and had a gold ring on his finger, and the other had on shabby clothing. The treatment the two received was based entirely upon their economic circumstances. The rich man was given a choice seat in the assembly while the poor man had to sit on the floor or stand.

James referred to the men coming into the "assembly." Actually he said synagogue. Some have felt this refers to a Jewish place of worship, perhaps one in which the Christians had taken complete control of the worship services. However, it is quite possible that this indicates that for a period of time Christians retained the name synagogue for their place of assembly.

Nothing is said about either of the two men other than to point out their economic situation. It is assumed that both were strangers and the ushers knew nothing about either of them personally as they were greeted and shown to their places. Nothing is said as to whether either of them was a Christian; therefore, we must conclude that the showing of favoritism was entirely due to outward appearances. James suggested three reasons why such behavior is evil.

Contrary to Faith

First, James made the point that showing partiality is contrary to faith *in* Jesus Christ. This is undoubtedly the correct translation, although many versions read "faith *of* our Lord Jesus Christ." James was talking about the faith which his readers have in Christ, not the faith Christ might have in them. Christ is called "the Glory." This word is the Shekinah of the Old Testament, which the rabbis taught was the visible glory of God's presence. By the use of the term, James indicated that Jesus was the full manifestation of the presence of God. It should be impossible to show partiality in God's presence.

Partiality is contrary to faith because it means that one is making distinctions among people whom God accepts as equals. Jesus, by his actions, showed God to be concerned equally with all men. He never turned away a poor man on the basis of his poverty or a rich man simply on the basis of his wealth. He never despised a Gentile or a Samaritan. He was willing to eat with immoral and wicked people as well as with the religiously righteous.

In his experience with Cornelius, the Roman army officer, Peter learned that there is no basis for partiality. After God granted him a vision (Acts 10:9–16), Peter willingly went to Caesarea. He entered the home of Cornelius and greeted him with the statement: "In truth I understand that God shows no partiality, but that in every nation he who reverences him and practices righteousness is acceptable to him" (Acts 10:34–35). Paul perceived that all distinctions were removed in Christ. "There is neither Jew nor Greek, there is neither slave nor free, there is neither male nor female; for you are all one in Christ Jesus" (Gal. 3:28, RSV).

Therefore, the man who judges on outward appearances is not being true to his faith. Faith sees beneath the surface and brings recognition of the oneness of brothers together in Christ.

James said men are guilty of becoming judges with evil thoughts when they show respect of persons. Instead of giving a true and right judgment, they are found to be making their decision on the wrong basis. Of course, we should never undertake to judge human worth, for we can only look on the surface and are not able to see the inner person. Thus, any judgment we might make is subject to possible error. Judgment must be left to God.

Yet how easy it is for us to slip into the habit of acting as judges and to make decisions about people on the basis of externals. We look at one person and feel he would make a wonderful addition to our church because he could make monetary gifts that would be helpful. Another man is so poor that any gifts he might give would not make any appreciable difference in the financial situation of the church. Unless we are careful, we will give more attention to the former and seek earnestly to lead him to become a member in preference to the second man.

Or, the difference might be that one person has the qualifications to be a good Sunday School teacher while the second could never hope to attain any position of leadership in the church. Which one do we strive to bring into the fellowship? Or the difference might be more subtle. Perhaps one gives the impression that he would fit in well with the current membership while the other man just does not appear to fit. Perhaps he belongs to the wrong social group, the wrong club, or does not have the right personality. When we make choices on the basis of such things, we are guilty of the very thing which James so strongly opposed. And unfortunately all of us are prone to such decision making.

Contrary to God's Appraisal

James noted that, in addition to being contrary to faith, the showing of partiality is also contrary to God's appraisal of men. "Has not God chosen those who are poor to the world to be rich in faith and heirs of the kingdom which he has promised to those who love him?" This agrees with the Old Testament. "In the Psalms 'the poor' is almost equivalent to 'the godly.' "[2] The desert community at Qumran (village of the Dead Sea scrolls) liked to refer to themselves as the poor.

Evidently there were not many rich among the early Christians. In the early decades, Christianity appealed mainly to the poor. There were some rich in the fellowship, but most converts were from the poor groups. This helps to explain the poverty of the Jerusalem church and the need for help to be sent to it (Acts 11:27–30). Poverty is the situation which lies behind Paul's statement to the Corinthians. "For consider your call, brethren; not many of you were wise according to worldly standards, . . . so that

---

[2] Mayor, op. cit., p. 87.

no human being might boast in the presence of God" (1 Cor. 1:26–29, RSV).

God's judgment does not always agree with that of man. Jesus was constantly criticized because he associated with the lower classes of his day. No one else could see the potential in these people. Jesus saw their individual worth and called them to follow him. God still confounds the judgment of the world. He is still concerned with all men. There are none so low—and none so high—that they are outside of God's concern, and his concern must be ours. Dare we go against God's appraisal in our outlook toward men? Only as we learn to look at others through the eyes of God can we begin to love them as God loves them.

We look at the wrong aspects of life when we make evaluations. We decide a person is rich because he has money in the bank or large amounts of property, but there are other things which constitute true riches. Who can measure the wealth of a fine family? What value can be placed on a good reputation? James called our attention to the item of intangible riches: The poor have been made rich in faith and this wealth is more enduring than money. Faith endures to eternity, but worldly things have only temporary worth.

Furthermore, the poor of this world become heirs of the kingdom. In identifying who these poor are who are to receive the kingdom, we need only to look at the words of Jesus: "Blessed are the poor in spirit, for theirs is the kingdom of heaven" (Matt. 5:3).

The ones who receive this kingdom are the ones who love God. There is no proper relationship with God unless there is love. We talk about fearing God and respecting him, but the chief attitude must be that of love. For he loved us and in return we must love him. Jesus pointed out that our love is an indication of the forgiveness of our sins (Luke 7:31–50). If we have really experienced forgiveness, we will love him.

Illustrated by Actions of the Rich

Partiality is illustrated in James by the action of the rich. The rich man of whom James spoke is guilty of two wrongs. First, he has oppressed the poor and brought him into court. In the verse 10 reference to the rich, it was assumed that the rich man was a believer. In these verses, it is probable that the rich men of whom James spoke are not believers. At least, James wrote as though they were not followers of Christ. Their usual conduct was to do anything that might increase their riches or their position of power and prominence. This would include the institution of lawsuits against others. Their behavior was anything but honorable. Why, then, James seems to have been asking, should excessive honor be shown to them when they come into the assembly?

The second wrong is that the rich blaspheme or speak evil of the "good name that was called upon you." The name is probably that of Christ or it may have been the term "Christian." This is perhaps a reference to the naming of Christ's name at the baptism of the believer. It was at this point in his experience that the name of Christ was literally called upon him. At the beginning of the Christian life, the believer comes under the influence and power of Christ. The name of Christ is called upon him, and he follows Christ from that point on.

It was the name of Christ which the rich spoke against, according to James. It would have been true with both rich Jews and rich Gentiles. The name of Christ was not one which was revered and honored by these people. Since they held such an attitude toward Christ, there was no excuse for Christians making a play for their favor.

James would not have approved the showing of partiality to any group. He realized that partiality is wrong because of the God whom he knew and the Christ whom he worshiped and served. Nor would James have us show resentment toward rich Christians. Christians who are rich through honorable means and are good stewards of their wealth are not among those of whom James spoke.

THE CHRISTIAN'S RELATION TO THE LAW (2:8–13)

Perhaps James expected someone to question his statements about the treatment of the rich. What if the concern shown to the rich man was really an expression of love? Would it be wrong to show such concern for him?

Motivation to Action

James implied that the action toward the rich was justified if it was an expression of love. He said the law, "You shall love your neighbor as yourself" (RSV), is proper and should be a guide for action. This is the royal law. This may indicate that the commandment is divine in origin. It is the law given by God and is a requirement for God's people who are a "royal priesthood" (1 Peter 2:9).

God has commanded us to have love for our neighbor. This commandment was given in the Old Testament (Lev. 19:18). On more than one occasion, Jesus emphasized its importance (Matt. 22:39; Mark 12:31). And difficult though it may be to keep, God expects his people to act out of love. It is not to be a halfhearted love. It must be directed to all persons, whether rich or poor, regardless of outward appearances or condition. All are our neighbors, and we must truly love them. This love is not to be simply a matter of emotion. God has not commanded us to like everyone or to be genuinely fond of every person. The love which is invoked here is a godly love—a deep concern for the person's spiritual and physical well-being.

Someone might claim that to receive the rich person in the assembly was obedience to the law of love. However, James seemed to feel that this was probably not the true motive, for they had despised the poor. They had shown partiality, and partiality is

sinful. There is no way to justify it before God. The individual
who practices it is exposed by the law as a transgressor. Such a
person will be called upon to give an account to God for his
action. He breaks God's requirements and must suffer the consequences.

Obedience to the Whole Law

Of course, one might argue that showing partiality is not a very
important matter after all, for there are other commandments that
are more significant. James did not agree with such an attitude.
On the contrary, the law is a unity. Either it is kept in its entirety
or the individual is guilty of being a lawbreaker. It may be that
he has disobeyed only one small item. Nevertheless, he is a breaker
of the law. The individual who shows partiality stands before God
as a violator of the law.

All law has been given by God. We cannot single out one commandment and say this came from God and another did not. Just
as God is a unity, the law stands as a unity. James pointed this out
with two commandments, those against murder and adultery. The
doing of either would make one a transgressor of the law.

This means that the believer is responsible completely to God
for all he is and all he does. As much as we might like to reserve
certain areas of our lives for self and take them away from the
control of God, it is impossible for us to do this. Breaking the law
makes one a transgressor whether it be in showing partiality or
committing murder. Both are actions which reflect the attitude
of the world rather than the attitude of Christ. Both are contrary
to God's revealed will and purpose. Neither of them is to find a
place in the life of the follower of Christ. "The conception of the
Law of God which James is condemning is the conception which
thinks of it as a collection of unconnected rules. That may fittingly
be regarded as a slavish conception, and the Law of Christ is a

law of liberty: it calls for the free manifestation in the outward conduct of the loving spirit within." [3]

God demands a high quality of life. "Thus speak and thus do as ones who are going to be judged by a law of liberty." Since this is a law the believer has voluntarily taken upon himself, he is under supreme obligation to be obedient to it. And since it is the only law which can bring true freedom, the obligation of proper action is much greater. It is this kind of law which will pass judgment on the individual. There can be no complaint that God is unfair, for we have chosen this for ourselves.

There is only one way of avoiding judgment from God, and that is by showing mercy to others. The one who shows no mercy receives no mercy. He who is merciful receives mercy. Thus "mercy boasts against judgment." Mercy must be shown without reservation.

We need to search our lives carefully and honestly to make sure that we do not show respect of persons. It is in such matters as these that we are most likely to offend. The "great" sins are easily recognized and usually avoided; but we are not so careful with other matters. James warned that partiality, as insignificant as it may seem, can nullify a believer's witness. We must strive with all our wisdom and energy to show our neighbor that we love him regardless of who he is, what he is, and how he may live. For it was such people whom Jesus loved while he was on earth, it was such people for whom he died, and it is to such people that he sends us as ambassadors bearing the message of the good news. It would be tragic if people rejected our witness because we could not overcome the tendency to be partial on the basis of outward conditions and appearances.

---

[3] Ross, *op. cit.*, p. 49.

4.
The
Relation
Between
Faith
and Works

With this portion of James (2:14–26) we come to that part of the writing which has caused many people in the past to feel that James does not rate consideration with the other great writings of the New Testament. When the author stated, "Was Abraham our father not justified out of works?" (2:21), it seemed that he had departed far from the New Testament concept of salvation by grace through faith.

Does James really teach that salvation is gained by works? On the surface this may well appear to be the situation. But before we join others in condemning James, let us take a closer look at his situation and what he was trying to do. This will give us a better opportunity to discover what he meant to say and the significance of his statements for us.

It is often claimed that James and Paul take completely opposite positions in the matter of faith versus works. Paul insisted that salvation is based entirely on faith and not on works. James seemed to place his emphasis on works, not on faith. However, on closer examination it appears that the differences between the two men are mainly a matter of words and emphasis rather than of basic disagreement in doctrine. Those who claim to find a basic difference between James and Paul differ with regard to which one wrote first. Some feel that Paul, in his writings, argued against James's position, or at least argued against a misunderstanding of James's teaching. Others feel that the author of this letter was writing against Paul's ideas or a misapplication of Paul's statements. The fact that there is such disagreement among scholars may lead one to wonder if perhaps there may not be some other answer to the entire question.

Our position in this study course book is to assume the early date for the writing of James. Therefore, the author could not have been arguing against Paul's doctrine of salvation through faith as presented in Galatians, Romans, and Ephesians for these had not yet been written. Furthermore, the book of Acts indicates that Paul and James were in basic agreement concerning how an individual is saved (Acts 15:13–21). It is possible that James's teaching was later misinterpreted by some who did not realize that faith and works are vitally related. Paul likewise faced this problem with some who felt that the doctrine of salvation by faith led to loose living (Rom. 6:1–4). But Paul's emphasis on salvation through faith is understandable without assuming that it was directed to a misuse of James's statements in this section of his letter.

The purpose of the writings in question must be remembered if they are to be correctly understood. Paul was setting forth the way in which men are saved. To a great extent, he was dealing with people who would be under the impression that salvation comes through obedience to the law. Some were even saying that faith in Jesus was not enough. There was a view among Jewish Christians that Gentiles, in addition to trusting Jesus, must become Jews and take upon themselves the obligation of the entire Jewish law, both moral and ceremonial. It was such ideas as these which Paul so strongly opposed. He wanted to make it clear that no man could be accepted by God through keeping the law. It was foolish even to try it. Hence, Paul gave his strongest emphasis to salvation by faith.

James was dealing with a different problem. With him, it was not the way of salvation that was in question. He would have agreed that man could be acceptable to God only through faith. But he was concerned to point out that faith is not true faith and cannot save unless it shows itself in the way the individual lives. Works are the natural and inevitable consequence of genuine faith. Works do not make a man acceptable to God, but they do show that the faith claimed is a valid faith.

Paul would have agreed with James's emphasis. It is true that he wrote the Ephesians: "For by grace are you saved through faith" (2:8). But he also insisted, "For we are his workmanship, having been created in Christ Jesus unto good works which God prepared beforehand in order that we might live in them" (2:10). Good works, as Paul used the term, are impossible for anyone who is not a Christian. And they are a necessity in the life of the believer. To this extent James and Paul are in complete agreement.

FAITH WITHOUT WORKS (2:14–17)

James first directed his attention to the individual who might claim to have faith but whose faith did not show itself in any outward expression. Undoubtedly there were people of such nature in the first century just as there are in our own day. One of the great hindrances to the spread of Christianity today is the individual who claims to be a Christian but does not show it in the life he leads. This is the man to whom James referred in these verses. What is the value of such faith? "James here speaks for the practical man of the present day who wishes to see some real difference in the life of a man who becomes a Christian." [1]

Without Spiritual Profit

At the center of all that is done is the spiritual content. We live in a materialistic society. Therefore, we have a tendency to place first emphasis on the material result of faith. James did not do this. Instead, he inquired first about spiritual profit. A man may boast all he wishes about his faith, but unless that faith shows itself in actions, can that kind of faith save him? The King James Version reads: "Can faith save him?" "At the time of this translation in 1611, it was not known that the definite article could be used as a demonstrative adjective, which is definitely its use here. The translation should be: 'Can that faith save him?'" [2]

There is no real conflict between Paul and James, only a different emphasis and a different problem being confronted.

Perhaps it would be well at this point to consider what is meant by the word "faith." It means so many different things when used by different people and in different situations that we must be careful to understand what we are speaking of when we use the term. For many people, faith is merely the intellectual acceptance of certain truths. Perhaps the average person outside the church thinks only of this when he hears the word "faith." However, the word itself is used in this way in the New Testament only a very few times if at all. Some suggest that James 2:19 is such a use.

Another meaning of "faith" is that found in Hebrews 11, where it has the meaning of assurance that the unseen is real. "Faith is the substance of what is hoped, the assurance of things which are not seen" (Heb. 11:1). This, of course, is a higher usage than

---

[1] Robertson, op. cit., p. 94.
[2] Billy Simmons, A FUNCTIONING FAITH (Waco, Tex.: Word Books, 1967), p. 72.

mere intellectual acceptance of something as truth. It accepts the reality of God and the spiritual. More is real than is known by the senses. However, this does not reach the depth of faith's meaning.

Faith, as commonly used in the New Testament, means the commitment of one's life without reservation to God in Jesus Christ. This is Paul's regular use of the term. Jesus used it in a similar way. It involves the acceptance of certain truths. It is the realization of who Jesus is and what he has done. It includes the sense of complete dependence upon God, but it also includes the acceptance of the lordship of Christ in the life of the individual. This is the only type of faith that is meaningful, and it is the only type of faith that the New Testament looks upon as having saving value. All other faith is weak and inadequate. This true faith will show itself in action. Christ is Lord of life. Self has been put aside and selfish ways are no longer pursued by the believer. He has become a new creation (2 Cor. 5:17). He has been born anew (John 3:3). Any other type of so-called faith is only a "dead" faith (James 2:17). And this new life will be evident in the person who has exercised such faith.

With this understanding of the meaning of faith, we can look at what James had to say in this passage. Can faith that does not issue in works save a person; that is, bring a man into a right relationship with God? James insists that it cannot. Perhaps he was remembering some of Jesus' own teachings. "If anyone desires to come after me, he is to deny himself, take up his cross, and follow me" (Matt. 16:24). "Not everyone who says to me, 'Lord, Lord,' will enter the kingdom of heaven, but he who does the will of my Father who is in heaven" (Matt. 7:21). Jesus repeatedly insisted that the right relationship with God must be demonstrated by obedience to the will of God. This is the very point James was making here. It is wrong for an individual to insist that he has saving faith unless this faith can be demonstrated in action. Faith that does not show itself cannot save. It is spiritually destitute.

Without Material Benefit

James well recognized that there would be some who would not be much impressed by the argument he presented in verse 14. Someone may have argued with James: "It is well and good to talk about saving faith, but how can anyone else know whether my faith saves?" James's reply was that saving faith must be practical. He used an illustration that is quite simple and very appropriate.

James called to mind a situation that must have been a familiar one in any first-century congregation—a poorly clothed and hungry person coming into the assembly. In such an instance, James asked, what value is there in words alone? It is easy to recognize a person's physical need, but mere recognition and expression of sympathy do not alleviate that need. It does no good to tell the person who is suffering for lack of warm clothing, "Go in peace; be warm," unless you help him find warm clothes and a source of heat by which to keep warm. It does no good to tell the person suffering the pangs of hunger, "Go in peace, be filled," when you do not provide food to ease his hunger.

These are very practical matters, but they are essential expressions of religion so far as James was concerned. Recall his statement in 1:27: "Religion that is pure and undefiled before God the Father is this: to visit orphans and widows in their affliction."

Jesus had taught that service to him is rendered by serving others (Matt. 25:31–46). Note especially these words: "Then he will say even to those on his left: 'Go from me, you accursed ones, into the eternal fire which has been prepared for the devil and his angels. For I was hungry and you did not give me anything to eat; I was thirsty and you did not give me anything to drink; I was a stranger and you did not welcome me; I was naked and you did not clothe me; I was sick and in prison and you did not visit me.' Then they also will answer and say: 'Lord, when did we see you hungry or thirsty or a stranger or naked or sick or in prison and not minister to you?' Then he will reply to them and say: 'Truly I say to you, inasmuch as you did not do it to one of these least, you did not do it to me'" (vv. 41–45). Is there not a close parallel between what Jesus said and what James insisted on? There is no value in expressions of concern that do not motivate action. Faith that does not result in action has neither material value nor spiritual value.

Without Life

James was very blunt when he stated: "Thus even faith, if it does not have works, is dead in itself." We would perhaps have been less dogmatic. We might have said it was weak or only a beginning faith, or we might have insisted that faith is not necessarily demonstrated by such outward acts. Certainly there are many people who are humanitarians. We can be grateful for the philanthropic concern of men who do their works out of simple concern for human need. Of course, such concern does not necessarily mean they are Christians. However, James would seriously question the actual situation of a person who claims to be a Christian and does not share such a concern for human need.

We are again reminded by James that while religion involves a personal relationship with God, it involves a relationship with our fellowmen also. Is this not an indictment of us who live in the most prosperous nation in the world with the highest standard of living ever achieved, when we are brought to the realization that much of the world is starving? In fact, many people in our own nation are hungry, cold, and uncomfortable. Millions of people go through life from birth to death and never know what it is not to be hungry. What does this say about our faith?

James insisted that true faith must show itself in action. It reveals itself in service to Christ, and service to Christ involves serving others. Any faith which does not show itself in this way is dead. This word means the opposite of life. Death can be used of those who are physically dead, and it is used of those who are spiritually dead, separated from God by sin in their lives. To be dead also means to be without power or significance or value. This seems to be James's principle idea here. Faith that is shown only by profession and not by action is without value and has no power to help others or to save the individual who professes such faith.

"Movement and action are the proof of life; thus any religious belief not attended by deeds, by the practical action for which God means it to be a vital impulse, is dead matter." [3] This claim demands that each of us look at ourselves honestly to see whether our faith gives any indication of life and vitality. Perhaps it is this demand, among other things, that has caused many readers to dislike the letter of James.

FAITH WITH WORKS (2:18-25)

James's discussion about the significance of faith would raise objections. There have always been those who would insist that faith and works are two separate matters. Could James sustain his position against the arguments of those who disagreed with him? The next several verses seek to support his position and show by argument and example what true faith really involves.

Shown by Works

At this point James adopted a style of argument that was quite common in his day. He wrote as though he were in a debate and was speaking to his opponent. At least this seems to be the best interpretation of the first part of verse 18. "But someone will say: 'You have faith and I have works.'" Perhaps this is a reminder that all things were looked upon as gifts from God, and God's gifts were not the same for all men. One man received one type of gift; another received another type. The objector (v. 18a) insisted that one man had received the gift of faith. This would not

[3] Moffatt, op. cit., p. 40.

necessarily involve the gift of works. The second man had received the gift of works, without any necessary relationship to the gift of faith. Such an argument must have been quite impressive in the early church with its insistence upon the free working of the Holy Spirit among believers.

The contrast is quite pointed. The statement made in verse 18 clearly contrasted two points of view. "You" and "I" are both emphatic. It is as though the objector were saying: You are on the one hand, and I am on the other hand. He saw no problem in such a division between faith and works. *You have faith.* It is as though the objector were saying to James, "Well and good! Since this is your gift from God, rejoice in it; but do not expect everyone else to be just like you. And do not be disturbed because you do not have works to go along with the faith. *I have works.* This also is well and good, and I will rejoice in that. But I do not demand that everyone have this same gift. For one man has one gift and another has a different gift." Thus did James seem to understand the viewpoint of those who took an "either/or" position on faith or works.

Possibly some undertones of Greek philosophy can be seen in this argument. We know that at a later time there were those who insisted upon a complete separation between the spiritual and material. The spiritual was viewed as totally good, and the material as completely evil. Thus, the only important thing would be the faith that was claimed. With those who held this view, there was no room for works, for anything that the body did was necessarily evil because the body was evil. Faith could never be shown by actions. It made no real difference whether actions were good or bad. In their understanding, what the body did could not affect the spiritual part of man. Therefore, for the believer there could be no such thing as sin because the spirit had been redeemed. The New Testament writers were in complete accord in opposing this dangerous heresy. If this is the background of the objector's argument here, James joins Paul and John in definite battle against it.

The rebuttal of James is quite pointed: "Show me your faith apart from your works and I will show you my faith by my works." Faith that is merely vocal cannot be true faith. It is not demonstrable. It cannot be shown. The challenge that James issued cannot be answered. How can one show the reality of faith except by the way in which he lives?

The faith shown through works principle is still operative today. There are many people who claim to be Christians whose lives appear no different than before their claimed conversion. While we are not, and cannot be, their judges, the question remains as to how they can justify their position when they do not demonstrate any change in life. Jesus referred to the conversion experience as a new birth (John 3:3). Paul said that any person who is in Christ is a new creation (2 Cor. 5:17). Many other passages from the New Testament could be cited in support of James's position that faith cannot be separated from the everyday activities of life. It is well to remember that these works must be obvious seven days a week if they are to be accepted as genuine.

So James claimed a faith that could be and would be shown by his life. "I will show you my faith by my works." Note that works do not take the place of faith. James has been wrongly accused at this point. Many have said that faith is almost overlooked by him. This is not true! He does not say that he will show you his works. Rather, he says, "I will show you my faith by my works." It is still faith that brings a man into a saving relationship with God in Jesus Christ. Faith is still the essential element in salvation, but James demanded that this be a true faith and a faith that can be seen in the life of the believer. It is not something to be kept hidden. It is not a faith that goes no further than its verbalization. It is a faith that changes all of life so that the change is obvious to the observer.

Again, it is not difficult to find support elsewhere in the New Testament for James's position. Paul emphasized the place of good works in Ephesians 2:10. John added his word in agreement: "He who says he is in the light and hates his brother is in the darkness until now" (1 John 2:9). "No one who abides in him practices sin; no one who habitually sins has seen him or known him" (1 John 3:6).

If logical reasoning could be convincing in such a discussion, the opponent of James should have been silenced by now. However, experience teaches that such argument is seldom so convincing. The issue quickly becomes emotional and reason has no point. It is easy to insist that James minimized the role of faith. To counter such a position, he once more returned to speak of faith that does not go beyond the mere intellectual acceptance of facts. He cited the traditional Jewish confession that God is one. This is not a direct quotation of the Jewish confession, but it is undoubtedly a reference to the words of Deuteronomy 6:4: "Hear, O Israel: The Lord our God is one Lord; and you shall love the Lord your God with all your heart, and with all your soul, and with all your might" (RSV). Such orthodoxy should be commendable. Every Jew was expected to repeat these words each morning and evening. It was his statement of faith concerning God. Jesus quoted the words and gave his approval to their truths. (See Mark 12:29-30; Luke 10:25-28.)

But the hollow repetition of these words was of no avail. Such meaningless repetition had not been sufficient in the days of the prophets who continually called the people back to repentance and trust in God. Even the demons could truthfully claim that they believed that God is one. It should not be surprising to realize that the demons would know this. In the Gospels we have evidence that they even recognized who Jesus was when men did not (Mark 1:24). While there may be much about demons which we do not understand, nevertheless James used them to indicate that even one so far removed from God as a demon could have a certain amount of insight into the nature of God.

The use of the word "belief" here may closely approximate the earlier reference to its use with regard to intellectual acceptance. The demons know about God, but this does not help them. On the contrary, "Even the demons believe and bristle." The word James used indicates the terror which comes from their recognition of the person and power of God. They are so afraid that their hair stands on end. They tremble or shudder in fright.

So, it is perfectly proper to confess that God is one. "You do well." But again James sought to point out how this in and of itself is never sufficient. The mere mouthing of orthodox phrases can never make a person acceptable to God. More is required. And this more is the work which gives evidence of the redeeming and sustaining power of true faith. It goes beyond words and it shows in action.

Shown by Example

It is always good if examples can be used to illustrate truths presented in argument. Are there examples of individuals whose lives would indicate that faith apart from works is dead and useless? Where would you look to find references to any man who claimed to have faith but with no works as a consequence? James did not seek such examples, but rather chose two persons whose lives would illustrate the close relationship between faith and works. These examples help us to understand that it is impossible to separate faith and good works.

As he prepared to introduce the first of these examples, James directly addressed the objector. He called him vain or foolish. It is not the idea of vain in the sense of vanity or pride. Instead, the word carries the idea of uselessness or worthlessness or emptiness. Thus, the one who argues from this point of view is foolish or empty-headed. He has missed the whole point of God's revelation.

He is pursuing the wrong course that will not and cannot lead to God. He is leaning upon a faith which is not strong enough to support him and present him acceptable to God. Such a man requires visible proof that his position is wrong.

James set out to show the objector that "faith apart from works is barren." The King James Version in this verse reads "faith without works is dead" as in verse 17. At this point the text followed in the King James Version is a later text. The older manuscripts support the reading "barren." To be sure, such faith is dead. But here James was concerned to show that it was useless or without fruit. The New Testament emphasizes that there will be fruit in the life of the Christian. Jesus said: "By their fruits you will recognize them" (Matt. 7:16). Paul listed the fruits of the Spirit as "love, joy, peace, long-suffering, kindness, goodness, faith, meekness, self-control" (Gal. 5:22–23). Faith which does not produce works of this nature is worthless and cannot bring redemption to the individual.

The demonstration of the relationship between faith and works is seen first in the life of Abraham. This man was the great religious figure in the minds of the people of the first century. Every Jew looked to him both as the father of their race and the beginner of their religion. It is true that Moses had a high place, but in many respects he was surpassed by Abraham. On more than one occasion Jesus had referred to Abraham in a commendatory way (Mark 12:26; Luke 16:19–31; John 8:39–58). Paul likewise referred to Abraham as the supreme example of faith and quoted Genesis 15:6 on two occasions (Rom. 4:3; Gal. 3:6), just as James did in verse 23 of this chapter.

This passage focuses attention upon the relation between faith and works. Since many have felt that Paul was writing in disagreement with James, or the author of this letter in disagreement with Paul, it is important to note what the author actually said. He did not rule out the role of faith in Abraham's experience. On the contrary, he insisted that faith and works went together in the life of this great man.

Part of our difficulty may be that James brings together two incidents in the life of Abraham that were widely separated in time. The statement from Genesis 15:6 was connected with the promise made by God that Abraham would have a son. The patriarch was much disturbed because he had no son and a slave born in his house would be his heir. God promised: " 'This man shall not be your heir; your own son shall be your heir' " (Gen. 15:4, RSV). God continued: " 'Look toward heaven, and number the stars, if you are able to number them.' Then he said to him, 'So shall your descendants be' " (Gen. 15:5, RSV). It is at this point that the great statement is made: "And he believed in the Lord; and he counted it to him for righteousness" (Gen. 15:6, KJV). Abraham's faith which was honored by God was faith that the promise of God would be fulfilled even though from a human point of view there was no hope of its fulfilment. If common sense and logic could mean anything, there was no hope that Abraham and Sarah could have a child. Abraham believed God in spite of the outward circumstances, and his great faith received its proper acclaim by later writers.

Paul emphasized Abraham's commitment to God and his promise. It was important for Paul because he was writing to people who were disputing about how a man could gain acceptance with God. Was a man acceptable by faith or by the works which he accomplished? The opponents of Paul, the Judaizers, insisted that it was by works of the law. It was necessary to become a Jew and fulfil the law of Judaism in addition to having faith in Christ. To many Jewish believers, faith was important, but it was not all. Paul reasoned with such persons that even Abraham was accepted by God through his faith and not through what he did. At this point in his life Abraham had done nothing about which he could boast. God accepted him because Abraham accepted and believed

God's promise. The same would be true of any person. He becomes acceptable to God only as he puts complete dependence upon God as Abraham did. Certainly Paul was not forgetting all that followed in Abraham's life in the way of good works. But all that followed was the result of his faith in God and not what gained for him God's acceptance.

"We are saved by our faith, not by our works; but immediately upon becoming children of God we feel compelled to express our new-found Christian joy by means of works. Paul says we are 'created in Christ Jesus for good works' (Eph. 2:10).

"Even though this great apostle denounced works as the condition of salvation, no one more adequately proclaimed them as the consequences of it. There is no greater means whereby one may express his faith than by a willing obedience to the commands of the Saviour." [4]

When we return to James's reference to Abraham, we discover that while he quoted the same verse, he was not thinking about Abraham's initial acceptance by God. He was writing, not on how to become a believer but, to persons who were already believers. Those to whom James directed his epistle knew that a man is saved through faith and not through works. Their problem was that they thought there was no place for works in the life of the Christian. Therefore, James did not emphasize the initial point of Abraham's faith and acceptance with God, but rather the incident that most clearly showed the depth and strength of that faith—his willingness to offer Isaac as a sacrifice to God. "James knew nothing of deeds or 'works of the Law,' i.e. observance of the ritual and ceremonial Law as constituting a claim for merit before God." [5]

Once more it is important to note the historical background of this incident. Abraham had an older son, Ishmael, born to Hagar

---

[4] William Wilson Stevens, DOCTRINES OF THE CHRISTIAN RELIGION (Grand Rapids: William B. Eerdmans Publishing Co., 1967), p. 226.
[5] Moffatt, op. cit., p. 43.

the maid of Sarah. God had informed Abraham that Ishmael was not to be his heir. Later, before Isaac was born, God had told Abraham: " 'Sarah your wife shall bear you a son, and you shall call his name Isaac. I will establish my covenant with him as an everlasting covenant for his descendants after him' " (Gen. 17:19, RSV).

No wonder the challenge to take Isaac and offer him as a sacrifice to God was such a significant event in Abraham's life. Here was the one through whom his descendants were to come. They were to be many. But now this son was to be slain. How was it possible for God to keep his promise? The faith of Abraham was great enough for him to believe that in spite of the events God would keep his promise. "By faith, Abraham, when he was tried, offered Isaac and he who had received the promises, to whom it had been said, 'In Isaac your descendants will be named,' offered his only son, because he reckoned that God was able to raise him even from the dead" (Heb. 11:17–19). The willingness of Abraham to present Isaac as a sacrifice to God was truly a work, but it was a work of faith. "You see that faith worked together with his works, and by his works faith was brought to maturity" (James 2:22).

What James seems to be insisting on is that if Abraham had not been willing to offer Isaac in keeping with God's command, it would have indicated there was something lacking in his faith. It would have been a barren faith and of no value to him. This is what James meant when he said that Abraham was justified out of works. The works gave proof of his faith. They did not replace faith but substantiated it. This is the whole point of what James sought to do in this passage.

In contrast with those who insist that faith and works can be separated and that one person may have faith and another works, James was quite certain that the two must go together. One cannot have faith without works, and equally one cannot have works without faith. The works of Abraham did not operate apart from faith but in cooperation with it. Without the prior experience of the patriarch in accepting God's promise, he could never have been willing to perform this great work of faith.

Thus, it is not incorrect to see in this account the fulfilment of the Scripture, "Abraham believed God and it was accounted to him for righteousness." It is in this context that verse 24 must be understood. Man is not justified by faith apart from works; that is, faith that does not issue in works is inadequate to bring the individual before God cleansed of sin. James did not mean that man is justified by works alone any more than he would agree that man is justified by faith alone. The two go hand in hand. Any attempt to separate them would meet with his strong opposition and be contrary to everything that God had revealed about himself and about man's need. Faith can no more exist alone than can works. For either of them to be vital, they must go together.

One further statement about Abraham needs notice. He was called a friend of God (Isa. 41:8). No higher praise could be given to any person. Jesus had spoken of his followers in the same way. "No one has greater love than this, that one give his life on behalf of his friends. You are my friends, if you do what I command you. No longer do I call you slaves, because the slave does not know what his master does; but I have called you friends because I have made known to you all the things which I heard from my Father" (John 15:13–15). Again the note of action is found here. We are his friends only as we obey, as we keep his commandments. Abraham was the friend of God because he obeyed God. He was the friend of God because faith and works operated together in his life. The same thing must be true of one today who claims to be a follower of the Lord Jesus Christ. Anything else is to run a foolish and unnecessary risk. Can faith separated from works really save a man?

It would be difficult to imagine an example further removed

from that of Abraham than the second one to which James made reference. He chose Rahab the harlot as an example of one who was justified by her works. Perhaps James chose to refer to her for the very reason of the vivid contrast between her and Abraham. It may be acknowledged that such a one as Abraham would show his faith by works, but what about someone who could not measure up to the high standard of the patriarch? James insisted that it made no difference who or what the person was. The same principle is true with every individual. Works as the consequence of faith are essential.

The story of Rahab is found in Joshua 2:1–21. Joshua had sent two men to spy out the city of Jericho in preparation for an attack upon it. The two men stayed in the house of Rahab. When the ruler of the city heard reports of this, he sent word to Rahab to deliver the spies. Instead of this, however, she hid them and sent back word that they had already departed. She later let them down over the wall of the city and sent them off to the hills to escape those who pursued them. But there was more involved in her action. Faith was the motivation of it. " 'I know that the Lord has given you the land, and that the fear of you has fallen upon us, and that all the inhabitants of the land melt away before you' " (Josh. 2:9, RSV). Also, her faith was shown as she said: " 'For the Lord your God is he who is God in heaven above and on earth beneath' " (Josh. 2:11, RSV). Only in the light of these statements did her action become possible. Only in the light of this faith could she do the works which James commended.

Once more it can be seen that it is not a situation of having either faith or works. Instead, both are viewed as working together. Just as Abraham showed his faith by his willingness to offer Isaac, so Rahab showed her faith by her willingness to hide the spies and make possible their escape, even at danger to her own life. Faith which would not have issued in such action would have been an ineffectual faith. It would have been barren and dead. James might well have repeated the words he used earlier with regard to Abraham: "You see that faith worked together with his works" (v. 22).

By these two examples James sought to establish his argument that faith alone, faith that does not issue in works, is not a vital faith. The two examples he used fully support his contention and solidify the truth that religion is practical in its service to God through service to men. His readers could not sit back and claim faith without showing it in their lives. Neither can we!

ANALOGY OF BODY AND SPIRIT (2:26)

James had one final word to say before leaving the subject of the relation between faith and works. He had made his point, but a final clinching analogy was offered. "For just as the body without spirit is dead, thus even faith without works is dead." It is quite possible that James was thinking at this point about the story of the creation of man. "Then the Lord God formed man of dust from the ground, and breathed into his nostrils the breath of life; and man became a living being" (Gen. 2:7, RSV). The word translated "spirit" in the passage in James can likewise have the meaning of breath. James would be saying that man became alive only as God breathed into him the breath of life. The body, then, is alive only as it is animated by the breath of God. Life is real only when there is spirit within man. Without a spirit there is only a corpse. There is no life.

The same thing holds true with regard to faith. Faith only has life when it is vitally connected with works, and the converse is equally true. If the connection between the two could be severed, then faith would have no more significance than a corpse. This is fully in keeping with all that James has said throughout this passage. He had begun with the question, "What is the profit, my brethren, if someone says that he has faith but he does not have works?" (2:14). James's answer is quite simple. There is no profit. Such faith, if it can be called faith at all, is inanimate and lifeless. It is of no more value than a mere corpse. Just as a body needs the life-giving spirit, so faith needs life-manifesting works to prove its reality. Faith without such works is dead. William Barclay sums it up thusly: "No man will ever be moved to action without faith; and no man's faith is real until it moves him to action. Faith and deeds are opposite sides of a man's experience of God." [6]

It would be well for each reader to pause and consider his own life. It is not uncommon for us to look at the lives of others and find their faults. But what about ourselves? Do our lives manifest the works which are the result of faith? Or are we among those whom James condemned as claiming faith but giving no evidence of it in their lives? What changes need to be made in our lives that we, like Abraham and Rahab, may show our faith by our works? We need to remember that faith and works operate together. For "works" in James means obedience to God in practical and ethical living, not just pompous ritual acts. They cooperate with one another. It is extremely dangerous to place all of our emphasis on faith to the neglect of works. It is perhaps even more dangerous to place all of our emphasis on works to the neglect of faith. Both faith and works have their place in the life of the Christian. No person is full-grown until both are a vital part of his experience. Jesus told his disciples: "Greater works than these you will do" (John 14:12).

"In James's day the moral crisis brought on by immature discipleship showed itself most vividly in a separation between believing and doing, faith and works. Is it not true that the church of our day faces a similar moral crisis, evident in a separation between what we profess and what we do? If this is true, then the book of James has come of age once again and speaks directly

---

[6] William Barclay, THE LETTERS OF JAMES AND PETER (Philadelphia: The Westminister Press), p. 92.

to us the same urgent message originally delivered to our fore-
fathers of almost two thousand years ago in this very same house-
hold of faith." [7]

What a tragedy it would be if we failed to heed the admonition
of this man of God when we are faced with the great needs of
our world today. Faith and works belong together and must never
be separated.

---

[7] Clifford Walter Edwards, CHRISTIAN BEING AND DOING (New York: Board
of Missions, The Methodist Church, 1966), pp. 64–65.

5.
The
Sin
of Selfish
Ambition

Ambition, like wealth, is not inherently evil. It can be a good quality when it is geared to the will of God. No one ever accomplishes anything worthwhile without ambition; but when ambition is motivated solely by selfish interests, it becomes a terrible evil. For then only self has importance. Everything is directed toward selfish advancement without regard to other people and organizations.

It was about such selfish ambition that James wrote in chapter 3. He knew that the Christian faith is of practical value in meeting every kind of difficulty in the life of man. James was stern in his warnings and advice for his day and for ours. His message is appropriate today, for men in 1970 are driven by worldly and selfish ambitions just as they were in the first century. This truth does not need documenting. All we need to do is look at our world in its chaos and travail, at our nation in its confusion and strife, at ourselves to see how often we act on the basis of self-interest instead of following God's purposes and designs.

ABUSE OF THE TEACHING PRIVILEGE (3:1–12)

The area where selfish ambition most manifested itself in the first century was in the widespread desire to teach. This may be surprising when we consider the difficulty that many of our churches have in finding enough people to take the responsibility of teaching in our educational programs. This may indicate a lack of dedication and concern on the part of many church members today. Even so, the problem James faced is still a modern problem although it may express itself in different forms. The widespread use of media of mass communication, the printed word, and parental duties make all of us susceptible to the misuse of words.

Responsibility of Teachers

"My brethren, be not many masters" (KJV). Unless we are careful, we may be misled at the very beginning of this discussion. This familiar translation may cause us to think of masters of slaves or of those who rule over men in other ways. This is not what James meant. The word used here for "masters" is translated "teachers" many times in the King James Version of the New Testament (John 3:2; Acts 13:1; and several other references in the Epistles). The word is regularly translated "teacher" throughout later versions of the New Testament. Even in the King James Version, the verb is translated "to teach." There is no question with regard to James's usage in this verse. "Not many of you are to become teachers."

In order to understand this reference, we must remember the situation. There are only a few references in the New Testament to teaching as a gift of the Holy Spirit to individuals. In some of these instances the gift of teaching is listed separately from other gifts (Rom. 12:7; 1 Cor. 12:28). However, in Ephesians 4:11 the gift of teaching is listed with that of pastor. The same man is referred to as pastor and teacher.

However, the idea of teaching as a separate and special function was not the ordinary one in that time. It is true that each Jewish synagogue had its teacher who instructed the young, and the synagogue had the teaching ministry as one of its basic functions. However, this appointed teacher was not the only person who taught. Far from it! The custom was that anyone might be invited to speak in the synagogue. An illustrious visitor or even a stranger could be called upon not only to read the Scriptures but to deliver the exposition of the Scriptures. Jesus regularly spoke and taught in the synagogues in Palestine. Paul was invited to teach in the synagogue wherever he went on his journeys, and he was glad to take advantage of the opportunities afforded him. He continued to teach in the synagogues until he was driven from them by the opposition of the Jews. Teachers, both official and unofficial, were numerous in Jewish life.

The same situation undoubtedly carried over into the early church. In the beginning all the churches had Jewish majorities, and we can assume that this was true of the churches addressed in this letter. Therefore, when James referred to teachers, he did not restrict his advice to individuals selected for an official and specific task of teaching. Instead, he had in mind the almost spontaneous effort by individuals to teach whenever they felt the leadership of God's Spirit. Evidently some of these teachers were motivated merely by the desire for recognition and honor. The role of teacher was one of honor and prestige. In one respect, they resembled the Pharisees whom Jesus condemned. They were anxious for the praise of men (Matt. 23:5–7).

We know there was considerable freedom in the meetings of the early churches. This is evidenced by the references Paul made to the disorder and confusion in the church at Corinth (1 Cor.

14). Not only were there many who would speak in the services, but there was no effort made by some of these to speak in a Christian spirit and with a concern for the welfare of the whole. This may have been a part of the problem confronted by James. Certainly there were those in the congregation who were actively seeking to be teachers without recognizing the accompanying responsibility. There was a widespread abuse of the teaching privilege. Men sought the task with inadequate preparation and from unworthy motives.

James had a word of severe warning for such people. They should realize that "we shall receive the greater condemnation" (KJV). While the word translated "condemnation" may have that meaning, it also has the meaning of judgment; and this rendering is given in the margin of some editions of the King James Version. It is the preferable translation. James did not mean that the teachers would be condemned just for teaching. He was trying to warn those who were seeking to be teachers that they would be held responsible by God for what they said.

The teacher has great influence. Think back concerning those persons who have been most influential in your own life. How many of them have been teachers at some level of your educational experience? The influence of teachers may be more far-reaching than that of parents. Therefore, James said, "We who teach shall be judged with greater strictness" (RSV). Instead of being a position to be lightly sought, the teaching position is one which is to be entered with a full realization of what God demands. We will be responsible to him for every word which is uttered (Matt. 12: 36–37). We may choose to ignore the responsibility, but we cannot avoid it. Note that James included himself among those who would be judged with greater strictness. He, too, was a teacher.

Let us add a word of caution at this point. This should not be a discouragement to any individual who feels that God would have him be a teacher. James was not writing about Sunday School teachers. If you feel that God can use you in the teaching ministry in your church, and you are willing to equip yourself for the task and accept the responsibility that goes along with it, you should follow his leading. In fact, if you feel that God would have you teach, you are violating your pledge to him if you refuse to do so. But remember that it is to be done for the glory of God and not to satisfy selfish ambition.

Control of the Tongue

One reason for James's strong caution to teachers is the problem of controlling the tongue. It is difficult at best. And when the individual is seeking self-advancement, it is even more difficult. James had already made reference to the tongue on two occasions in this letter. In 1:19 he said: "Be quick to hear, slow to speak." And in 1:26 he said: "If anyone thinks that he is religious and does not bridle his own tongue but deceives his own heart, the religion of this man is vain."

We need not rely on the words of James alone to realize the difficulty of controlling the tongue. How often we have seen the truth demonstrated in our own experience. It is easy to speak without thinking. Many times we have spoken and then wished that we could call the words back again. James's statement that the man who does not offend in what he says is perfect and able to control his entire body may be an overstatement for the sake of emphasis. One writer has said, "If anywhere under the sun there could be found a man who had perfectly bridled his tongue, he would be a perfect man, or a man who is spiritually mature." [1] It would be possible for someone to control his tongue quite well and yet be guilty of sin in other areas of life. Yet we recognize the truth of what James said. It is easier to sin in word than in action, and all of us are prone to such sin.

We know there is no perfect man. Those who claim to be

[1] Ross, *op. cit.,* p. 59.

perfect are only deceiving themselves. Paul pointed out that all have sinned (Rom. 3:23). John stated: "If we say that we do not have sin, we deceive ourselves and the truth is not in us" (1 John 1:8). So James did not exaggerate when he said, "We all stumble many times." Unfortunately, this is the story of human life. It has been the experience of man since Adam, and we are no different than were our ancestors. It does no good to try to deceive ourselves. Sin is still a human reality, and it must be recognized and confessed before it can be overcome.

Sin expresses itself in many ways and in many forms. Sin is frequent in the words which pass from our lips. James said: "If anyone does not stumble in word, he is a full-grown man, able to bridle even his whole body." Our control of speech is a good indication of our control of the rest of the person. We are familiar with some of the more obvious ways in which men sin with their language. We are offended by the filthy words that are a common part of the speech of some. We may be shocked by the cursing which is a part of the vocabulary of others. These are quite common faults, and are unbecoming to a Christian, a new man created in Christ Jesus.

But is this the only aspect of speech with which James was concerned? Or was it profane and filthy language about which he was writing? The problems in James's day were quite different from our own, and yet they represent the things in which believers today may be easily entrapped. The recipients of this letter would not have given serious thought to taking the name of God lightly, but they did not hesitate to pronounce curses upon men (v. 9). They heaped abuse upon those who opposed them. Their words gave expression to their sharp anger and bitter jealousy. Instead of being used to express Christian love, words were being used to express unchristian anger and hatred.

Even though we may not share the contentious and excitable spirit of the people of the first century in that part of the world, nevertheless we, too, discover that we allow ourselves to be betrayed by our speech. We give expression to our anger, even within the church. Is it not true that most of the trouble which occasionally plagues our churches comes because of the careless or unwise speech of some individual? Most of the ill-feeling between individuals is the result of words rather than action. No wonder James spoke of the tongue as an unstable evil.

There are other ways in which we err with our words. How easy it is to pass on that juicy piece of gossip which we have just heard. One scholar has put it this way: "A garrulous man is a bore at best, while a woman with a sharp tongue is a terror to the community." [2] It is convenient many times to tell a lie, and we justify it by speaking of it as merely a white lie. We say behind a person's back things which we would not dare say to his face. It would not be an exaggeration to say that more trouble is caused in our world by the spoken word than by anything else. If we could only learn to control our tongues, perhaps we would deserve to be called mature people. But how hard it is!

Someone might ask why James placed so much emphasis on the tongue. It is such a small part of the body. In a day when emphasis is placed upon great moral issues such as murder, war, sex, and drugs, why should anyone be worried about such a small and insignificant part of the body? The answer, of course, is that often the little things are the most important and exercise control over the bigger things. James illustrated this with two examples.

The first of these illustrations is the horse. How does one control a horse? He is so large and strong, but there is one way in which control can be exercised. Put a bit in the mouth of the horse, and with this bit one can guide the horse and control all of his actions. It does not matter that he is stronger, that he is much bigger. The small bit gives the rider the power to determine the direction of the horse.

---

[2] Robertson, *op. cit.*, p. 111.

Then James referred to the ship. It is far greater in size than the horse. It is far larger than the man who sails in it. It faces powerful forces in the waves and the winds. Yet one man can control the ship by the use of the little rudder. He can make the ship go in whatever direction he pleases by simply moving the rudder. The rudder is a little thing, but one that has power over something far larger than it is. The ships of James's day on the Sea of Galilee, or even the Mediterranean Sea, would not be comparable in size to the vast oceangoing vessels of our day. This merely emphasizes the contrast for us. The rudder is still small in comparison to the rest of the ship, and the course of the ship is controlled by the hand of the helmsman on the rudder.

Having shown the significance and power of little things, James gave his attention once more to the tongue. "Thus even the tongue is a little member and boasts great things." The tongue is small, but its power and influence are out of all proportion to its size. It does boast great things, but this boasting is not idle or false, for the power it exercises is beyond measure. Just as the bit guides the horse and the rudder controls the ship, so the tongue controls the life. It is the master of the individual.

To be sure, we need to realize that James was looking only at the outward situation at this point. We know that the tongue is not an independent thing in our bodies. It only follows the direction of the will and intellect. It does not act on its own, although sometimes it may give this impression. Yet we can understand the writer's point. We cannot see or hear the will and the intellect of the individual. It is the words which we hear, and they cause the damage. We must make certain that we do not sin in our speech.

Evils of the Tongue

The tongue is little and powerful. It is evil and the cause of much harm. James emphasized this: "What size fire kindles what

size wood!" Today's English Version translates it this way: "Just
think how large a forest can be set on fire by a tiny flame!"[3]
One who lives in an area where grass and forest fires are a yearly
summer hazard can appreciate what James said. It only takes one
spark to set off a conflagration that may consume thousands of
acres of timber. The financial loss from fires each year is stagger-
ing, not to mention the danger to life; and most of these fires
are started by the carelessness or the purposeful intent of man.

"And the tongue is a fire." The tongue is a tiny spark, but it
starts a great conflagration. It is so small and may appear so innocent. When properly controlled, like fire, the tongue is of in-
estimable benefit to man. But when improperly restrained, when
it gets out of control, the damage it can cause is beyond imagination. Perhaps the picture of a forest fire was "suggested by the
sight of an excited audience in some place of meeting . . . the
noise of tongues, and gesticulation of the arms . . . might most
aptly be compared to a forest fire; the tongue of one speaker has
set ablaze all the inflammable material which controversy brings
into being."[4]

What a loss there would be to mankind if we could not speak.
How difficult it would be to communicate with one another. The
tongue was intended by God to be a blessing to man, and it can
be. But like everything else that God intended as a blessing, the
tongue has been perverted through sin and has been made a curse.
That which was intended for good has become evil. Just as fire
provides heat and light but can also destroy, so the tongue is vital
in our relationships with one another—but it also can be destructive. It is a fire in every sense of the word.

While the general sense of James is clear, commentators are in

[3] GOOD NEWS FOR MODERN MAN, THE NEW TESTAMENT IN TODAY'S
ENGLISH VERSION (New York: American Bible Society, 1966). Used by per-
mission.
[4] W. E. Oesterley, "The General Epistle of James," EXPOSITOR'S GREEK
TESTAMENT, ed. W. Robertson Nicoll (Grand Rapids: William B. Eerdmans
Publishing Company, 1951), p. 451.

disagreement about some of the details of verse 6. There are problems of punctuation as well as of translation. Realizing that the earliest manuscripts had no punctuation marks, it seems best to translate verse 6 in this manner: "And the tongue is a fire. The tongue is constituted a world of unrighteousness among our members. It stains the whole body and sets on fire the wheel of nature, and it is set on fire by hell." A number of things call for attention in this verse.

First, we note that the "tongue is constituted a world of unrighteousness." Most translations state, "is a world of unrighteousness." The Greek verb translated "is" in this verse, though it is used thusly in at least one other place, usually carries the idea of making something to be different from what it was before. James said the tongue was not designed or made by God to be evil. Like everything else in the body, it is neutral, dependent upon the will and wishes of the man. Only as it has been misused has it become an unrighteous world among the members of the body. Therefore, the tongue was not made to be evil, but it becomes evil and can cause evil.

The second phrase to which we direct our attention is "a world of unrighteousness" ("iniquity," KJV). This means an unrighteous realm. The same type construction is found in Jesus' reference to the mammon of unrighteousness (Luke 16:9), meaning unrighteous mammon. Thus, James said the tongue has become an unrighteous realm in our bodies. The term world or realm is regularly used in this writing as being in opposition to God. So the tongue has become within our bodies a realm which is set up in direct opposition to God and his goodness. This was not due to God's action in creation but man's involvement in sin.

The third expression is that the tongue "stains the whole body." We have already had occasion to notice how James liked to pick up a word used previously. "Stain" is the same word that is found in 1:27 where James said that a second aspect of true religion is that the individual "keep himself unspotted from the world." The believer must be without spot or stain.

While we might be inclined, as were the religious Jews of the day, to think that stain would come from outward contacts, James was true to the spirit of Jesus with his recognition that stain comes from within. Jesus said: "Do you not realize that everything from without which enters man is not able to defile him? . . . But that which proceeds out of the man defiles the man" (Mark 7:18-20). That which comes from within gives indication of the true inner nature of the person. James insisted that the words which come from the mouth give a clear picture of what is within the person. The stain of which James spoke is not acquired from externals primarily. It comes from within the heart. The tongue expresses the thoughts of the heart and the true nature of the man.

A fourth thing we note is that the tongue "sets on fire the wheel of nature" ("course of nature," KJV). Commentators are not in agreement as to what James meant. It seems unlikely that he was making any reference to a cyclical view of life which was so common among the Greeks of the day. Nor does it seem to be simply a reference to the birth of the individual. Instead, he referred to the totality of life. The use of the word "wheel" may be due to the picture of a flaming chariot wheel. The wheel is set on fire by the heat of the axle which has not been properly lubricated and becomes red-hot. The axle catches fire and the entire wheel burns. So, the tongue is a fire, and it spreads to engulf all of life.

The final phrase in this verse is that the tongue "is set on fire by hell." The New Testament word for hell is derived from the word used to refer to the valley of Hinnom. This was at one time the place where human sacrifices were offered to Molech. When the Israelites gained possession of Jerusalem, this valley was made the city dump. Into it was thrown the refuse of the city, perhaps along with the bodies of executed criminals. The fires burned in this valley without ceasing. "Hell is the rubbish heap of the Universe—is that the idea suggested?"[5] Thus, it portrayed the extreme torment and agony which were thought to be associated with the eternal punishment of the wicked. The flames of the valley pictured the eternal flames of hell.

The tongue is set on fire by hell. The root of the trouble lies with the activity of Satan. As he is the originator of all sin, so he is the one who has made the tongue an instrument for evil. The connection between hell and Satan is that hell is recognized as his abode and the place of eternal torture for him and his followers.

In verse 6 James pointed out the evils of the tongue. The tongue, created by God for good, has been made into an instrument of evil by Satan. It has been set on fire by the fires of hell itself, and the tongue is capable of infecting and destroying all the rest of the body. It is small, but its influence and power are great. For this reason every person must seek to bring this member of the body under complete control.

James emphasized how difficult it is to control the tongue. It is far easier to tame wild animals. Perhaps he was thinking back to the statement in Genesis 1:28: " 'Be fruitful and multiply, and fill the earth and subdue it; and have dominion over the fish of the sea and over the birds of the air and over every living thing that moves upon the earth' " (RSV).

While on the surface James's statement may appear too broad, nevertheless it is true that man has tamed almost every type of creature there is. All types have been taught to obey man and to respond to man's orders. Contrast this with the problem of the tongue. "But the tongue, no one of men is able to tame." In this statement, the emphasis is placed on the tongue. While man has learned to control his world, and this is far more evident today than it was in the first century, still he has not learned to control

---

[5] Ross, *op. cit.*, p. 62.

his tongue. He can do amazing things with his body, even to the point of controlling weight and correcting many defects, but he has not gained control over his tongue and his will.

Some writers feel that the secondary emphasis upon the phrase "of men" is significant. They point out that certainly no man can control his tongue, but God can. And the individual who is fully surrendered to God can tame his tongue just as he tames everything else about his person. This is quite true, but it is unlikely that this is the point James was trying to make.

The tongue is "an unstable evil, full of deadly poison." This is a harsh description of the nature of the tongue. It is unstable or restless; it is continually in action. The word "unruly" in the King James Version is based on a manuscript reading which differs in only two letters from the earlier manuscripts. However, the reading found in later translations is likely to be correct. True, the tongue is unruly, but this has already been stated; and James does not so repeat himself. Consider this translation: "But no human being can tame the tongue—a restless evil, full of deadly poison" (RSV).

The tongue is also "full of deadly poison." The serpent was thought to carry poison in its darting tongue. So man's tongue brings death. How much character assassination is done by the spoken word! James's picture is true to life.

The tongue is also contradictory. "With it we bless the Lord and Father, and with it we curse men who have been made according to the likeness of God. Out of the same mouth proceed blessing and cursing." The statement "Lord and Father" is unique in the New Testament. Nowhere else are these two terms joined together in reference to God. (The King James Version translation "God" follows a later change in the text which brought the statement into line with other references to God.) The term Lord emphasizes the power and majesty of God. The word Father emphasizes his love and compassion.

Men would and should bless God. This means to praise and speak well of him and to him. The opposite of this is to curse. Cursing may not have been looked down upon in Jewish life as much as it is today. However, we can be confident that it was never encouraged or tolerated in Christian circles. The basic reason that it is wrong to curse a man is that man is made in the image of God. Therefore, when you pronounce a curse upon some man, in a sense you are pronouncing the same curse upon God because that man was made in God's image. While the image of God in man may be marred, it has not been destroyed. We may seek all we wish to get around this statement, but it remains before us. There are no exceptions. All men are made in God's image; therefore, we must not be guilty of calling down evil upon any man because in doing so we curse God.

Therefore, it is contradictory for blessing and cursing to come forth from the same mouth. "My brethren, it is not fitting for these things thus to happen." James made his statement as mild as possible and further tempered it by associating himself with the readers as their brother. Nevertheless, the rebuke is still there. For such cursing to come from the same mouth that has pronounced a blessing upon God is a paradox. But this is the picture of "life in the religious world of the day, where teachers and preachers uttered lofty sentiments and voiced spiritual truths before their congregations, and also gave way to bitterness in controversy, even cursing their opponents. . . . Talk about religion among ordinary members of the church might be wholesome, but the same people were guilty of spitefulness and scandal in social intercourse, inflaming the passions of others by cruel, careless words or poisoning the mind by insinuations." [6]

Even nature shows this to be wrong. Fresh and bitter water do not flow from the same spring. A fig tree does not produce olives, nor does a grapevine produce figs. All of this is contrary to nature.

---

[6] Moffatt, op. cit., pp. 50–51.

It is also contrary for man both to curse and to bless. For the words that come forth from the mouth are a true barometer of the condition within. You cannot bless God and curse those made in his image. John said: "If anyone says 'I love God,' and hates his brother, he is a liar; for he who does not love his brother whom he has seen, cannot love God whom he has not seen" (1 John 4:20). If one both curses and blesses, he is flaunting hypocrisy, for obviously the words of blessing are not sincere.

FALSE WISDOM AND SELFISH AMBITION (3:13–18)

In the previous paragraph (3:1–12), James spoke to those who would teach. It is quite likely that he had these same teachers in mind when he made reference to the wise and understanding in verses 13–18. Undoubtedly there were many in the churches who made claims to such achievements. It is easy and pleasant to claim wisdom, but such self-proclaimed wisdom is seldom true wisdom. True wisdom never calls attention to itself, never displays itself for personal profit. The man who is wise and understanding "is to show out of his good manner of life his works in the meekness of wisdom."

Once more we are called back to James's insistence that the good qualities of life must be shown in practical ways. It is not enough to boast of wisdom; it is not enough to claim to have understanding. These qualities, if real, will manifest themselves in the type of life lived. The wise man shows his works, not his wisdom.

James had earlier said that wisdom comes as a gift from God, and if a man lacks it he is to ask God that it might be given to him (1:5). The term for the wise man (3:13) is that which is regularly applied to one who teaches. The man "endued with knowledge" (KJV), who has understanding, is the one who is capable of instructing others. But all of this must show in a good manner of life. In the seventeenth century, the expression "conversation" (KJV) meant all of life. But language changes with the generations. Conversation today is restricted to the exchange of words between people and does not refer to other aspects of life. James was far more inclusive in his instruction. All of life is involved, not just the spoken words.

The wise man will show his works in the meekness of wisdom. This is a true quality of wisdom. Meekness is the opposite of pride and self-esteem. It is the quality of a life dedicated to a master. Jesus said: "Blessed are the meek, for they shall inherit the earth" (Matt. 5:5). Any person who claims wisdom or understanding and lacks meekness is puffed up by false wisdom and has not received the true wisdom which comes from God. For "the only really wise man is he who places God in the center of his life, who serves Christ as Lord and Master, who keeps the intellect in subjection to the will of God." [7]

The Source of False Wisdom

Just as true wisdom shows itself by the person's manner of life, so does false wisdom show itself. It is manifest in "bitter envying and strife" (KJV). The first term can be better translated "bitter jealousy." Jealousy is our word "zeal" and can have either a good or bad meaning. It was used in a good sense in John 2:17 to refer to Jesus' zeal for the Temple. In Romans 10:2, Paul also used the word to refer to the zeal of the Jews. It is used in an evil sense in Galatians 5:20 and Acts 13:45 as well as numerous other places in the New Testament. The use of the adjective "bitter" makes it clear that the jealousy referred to by James is an evil quality. James had more to say about this jealousy and strife or selfish ambition in verse 16. However, where these qualities are found there is no reason to boast about any supposed wisdom. Such boasting would be a lie against the truth because the character of life obviously is contrary to true wisdom.

---

[7] Robertson, *op. cit.*, p. 126.

Because of its source, false wisdom is a dangerous and deadly thing. "This wisdom does not come down from above, but it is earthly, unspiritual, demonic." We need to remember that wisdom cannot be equated with intelligence or knowledge. One may have great intelligence and still have little or no wisdom. One may have acquired great knowledge and secured a fine education, but this is no guarantee that he has wisdom. True wisdom comes only as a gift from God (1:5). And this wisdom shows itself in meekness and proper life as James has already insisted. Any other kind of life shows that the wisdom claimed has come from the domain of Satan rather than from God.

James used three terms to describe this false wisdom. The first is that it is earthly. This signifies that it is concerned with worldly things rather than with man's relationship with God. The term is used infrequently in the New Testament. In his conversation with Nicodemus, Jesus spoke of earthly things as being distinct from heavenly things such as the new birth (John 3:12). Paul wrote about our earthly house with reference to the body designed for life on this earth (2 Cor. 5:1). He also wrote of earthly bodies in contrast with heavenly bodies (1 Cor. 15:40). The usage closest to that of James's is Philippians 3:19, where Paul wrote of those who mind earthly things.

It is clear that the term is used to point out the contrast with the higher stages of being which are referred to as heavenly. James spoke of a wisdom that is related only to earthly matters and does not concern itself with that which is most important.

The second term used by James to describe false wisdom is difficult to translate. It is sometimes translated "sensual" (KJV) or "unspiritual" (RSV). The term refers to the natural man as he is considered separate and apart from the working of God's Spirit. Paul used the term three times to distinguish the present body from the resurrection body (1 Cor. 15:44,46). The closest usage is 1 Corinthians 2:14. "A natural man does not receive the things of the Spirit of God, for they are foolishness to him; and he is not able to know them because they are spiritually discerned." Thus, the unspiritual or sensual man is the natural man. He is man without benefit of God's redemption and mercy. False wisdom is totally unrelated to God and his Spirit.

James further described false wisdom with the strongest term of all: demonic, devilish. This particular Greek word occurs nowhere else in the New Testament, but it is closely related to the common words which refer to demons. False wisdom has its ultimate source in Satan and is communicated to men by his servants. Instead of working for the good of the possessor, false wisdom works against him. Instead of helping men, it harms them.

Results of False Wisdom

Anything which emanates from hell is certain to have evil results. James referred to the qualities of life which characterize false wisdom as bitter jealousy and selfish ambition. The individual with such wisdom does not seek to serve God but self. He does not seek the welfare of others but his own welfare.

Such evil attitudes should never be found in the life of any Christian, but experience teaches us that such qualities have a way of creeping into our lives. How often within a church some individual seeks the position of prominence. And if someone else receives honor, he becomes fiercely jealous. Words are spoken and things are done which are not fitting for one who would exemplify Christian love. The spirit of unity within the fellowship is broken and the cause of Christ is hindered. All of this happens because someone suffered hurt to his self-centered pride.

There is no way of estimating how much harm is done by selfish ambition which involves strong rivalry. As has already been suggested, ambition is necessary if anything worthwhile is to be accomplished; but all ambition must be kept under the control of the Spirit of God. When guided by the human impulse, or worse by the spirit of Satan, ambition can bring about terrifying results.

Two of the results of jealousy and selfish ambition are "disorder and every evil practice." Disorder is a strong word. It is associated with wars in Luke 21:9. Thus, it is close in meaning to anarchy. Paul associated it with other types of quarreling and controversy which he feared might break out when he returned to Corinth (2 Cor. 12:20). Such disorder prevailed in the Corinthian church when prophets and others in the church did not keep their gifts under restraint (1 Cor. 14:33). And the Corinthian Christians seem to have prided themselves on worldly wisdom.

Even worse, of course, would be "every evil practice." False wisdom, inspired by the devil, results in sin and evil. No man can dare depend upon himself. To do so is to be certain of failure. It is when man thinks that he is at his best that he most frequently fails himself and his God. Dependence must be placed upon God alone. Human wisdom cannot cope with the situations which we face. A casual look at our world today should make us well aware of this. While man has achieved phenomenal things in the scientific sphere, he has been unable to establish control of the world's social, economic, and political conditions. Therefore, man's achievements have all too often been used to harm rather than to assist. This is the work of false wisdom.

Contrast with True Wisdom

An awareness of James's propensity for being practical would lead us to expect him at this point to show that true wisdom reveals itself in practical ways. He has no room in his thoughts for theoretical knowledge or wisdom. If anything is real, it must show itself in the way the individual lives. This can be said of false wisdom, and it is equally true of the wisdom which is from above.

James listed several positive aspects of true wisdom. It is pure, peaceable, gentle, compliant, full of mercy and good fruits. Coming only from God, true wisdom manifests itself in purity of life. It avoids not only the gross sins but all sins. Purity of life is an essential quality for the man of God. Jesus said: "Blessed are the pure in heart, for they shall see God" (Matt. 5:8). The word for pure that Jesus used is a different word, but the thought is much the same.

Wisdom leads one to be peaceable. Again a Beatitude is recalled: "Blessed are the peacemakers, for they shall be called sons of God" (Matt. 5:9). This is the opposite of the bitter jealousy and selfish ambition which James said were the characteristics of false wisdom. The wise man is anxious to live at peace with his fellowman. This is a sign of wisdom.

Wisdom leads to gentleness in life. This word carries the idea of that which is fitting or fair or equitable. The life characterized by wisdom does not deal harshly with others.

The man who has wisdom is compliant. This means "easy to be entreated" (KJV), or "open to reason" (RSV). Such a person does not have a closed mind. He can be approached and be expected to listen to all sides of a question before making up his mind.

Wisdom leads to mercy and good fruits. In 2:13 James had referred to the place of mercy in the life of the believer: "For judgment is without mercy to him who does not show mercy." The individual who does not show consideration, love, and kindness has no right to claim to have received wisdom from God. Wisdom leads to the proper kind of fruit bearing.

The last two words used to describe the wisdom which comes from above are negatives. Such wisdom is without indecision ("without partiality," KJV) and without hypocrisy. The first of these terms recalls the man referred to in 1:6. He was the man who doubted, who could not make up his mind. There is no room for uncertainty or indecision in the person who has this wisdom which comes from God. He has God's leadership, and he follows it without doubt and without question. "The man whose conduct is governed by worldly wisdom is apt to be shifty—what he himself would call politic. He sets his sails to the prevailing wind; speaks well of men today of whom he spoke ill yesterday—not because the men themselves are better than they were, but because yesterday he could get nothing by speaking well of them, and today he can." [8]

True wisdom is also without hypocrisy. It is sincere. There is no playacting. It is not a game. There is no room for attempted deceit. Wisdom gives a fair and honest picture at all times.

It is easy to see in all of this discussion of true wisdom that James was much influenced by the book of Proverbs, especially the marvelous picture of wisdom in chapters 8 and 9 of that book. He was also familiar with much of the other Wisdom Literature of the Jews, especially the Wisdom of Solomon and Ecclesiasticus. No attempt has been made in this writing to trace the parallels between James and these writings although they are many in number.

James's final statement in this paragraph picks up the idea of peace again. "The fruit of righteousness is sown in peace for those who make peace." This may mean the fruit which *is* righteousness or the fruit which righteous living produces. In either case, righteousness is directly related to peace. There can be no true righteousness among those who do not seek peace and live in peace. Here is an essential quality of the wise man. He does not stir up strife. Instead, he lives in peace and seeks to bring peace among others.

In an age too often characterized by violence, in a generation which has known no true peace, we have come to a time when we assume that internal revolution and violence and war between nations are the normal situations. It is difficult for us to envision a world free of such strife. It is hard for us to catch again the

---

[8] Dale, *op. cit.,* p. 118.

great purpose of God and his demand that his people be peaceable. Perhaps if we would seek to make peace a reality within our own fellowships, we could make an impact upon the world and be used of God to draw people closer to him. Righteousness can prevail in the world only as it prevails in the hearts of individual Christians and in their fellowships. We need to pray for this wisdom which comes from above, and we need to be bold in expressing this wisdom in the ways which James mentioned.

6.
Warnings
Against
Spiritual
Failure

Having spoken of peace at the close of chapter 3, James seems to have been reminded that all was not peaceful in the churches. This may surprise us, for we tend to idealize the first century. We find it difficult to imagine that people in those days had problems so similar to ours. We have sometimes thought that the enthusiasm of the first days—the great faith of those who had seen Jesus in the flesh, and the faith of those who had been converted through their witness—would cause them to avoid the common sins which curse men today.

Unfortunately, this was not the case. Of course, much of the New Testament would never have been written, including the letter of James, if the early Christians had been perfect, for these writings were concerned with the difficulties faced by the first believers. Those people were not perfect, and sometimes we are shocked to discover some of the conditions which prevailed. Reading the Corinthian correspondence of Paul should open our eyes to their imperfections and warn us about our own.

Someone will say that some evil practices might be expected in a church composed of Gentiles, people who were converted out of paganism and who brought some of their pagan practices over into the early churches. But James wrote to Jewish believers, and their situation would be different. The standard of morality among the Jews was far higher than it was among the Gentiles. Certainly they would not have the moral problems which affected others, but we need only read Romans 2 to realize that the Jews also had ethical difficulties. They brought these practices over into their new faith. Therefore, the congregations to which James addressed his letter were imperfect; they had moral and ethical faults.

It has been suggested that James had been greatly influenced by conditions in Judea. Strife about the law was bitter. The Zealots were working feverishly to stir up rebellion and murder. This may have influenced James's language, but we must assume the conditions about which he wrote were true throughout the churches, among converted Jews as well as the unconverted.

"These verses reveal an appalling state of moral depravity in these *Diaspora* congregations; strife, self-indulgence, lust, murder, covetousness, adultery, envy, pride and slander are rife; the conception of the nature of prayer seems to have been altogether wrong among these people, and they appear to be given over wholly to a life of pleasure." [1] The picture does look dismal. Even among early Christians the improper use of words is understandable. Wherever there are people we expect to find gossip and selfish ambition. But were the strains of evil so strong and so deep-seated that there could be murder, wars, and fightings among them? All of these problems reflect the spiritual failures of some of the readers. James issued sharp warnings against these failures.

---

[1] Oesterley, *op. cit.,* p. 456.

AGAINST IMPROPER DESIRE FOR GAIN (4:1–3)

The active and energetic seeking for material gain led to all sorts of strife among the people. The terms used to describe this strife were "wars and fightings." These two words are closely related but there is a difference. The first refers to the settled enmity which is involved in warfare. The second term refers to the excitement and feeling which leads to the outbreak of battle or fighting. Of course, James was not referring to war on an international scale. He was concerned about the relations which prevail between individuals within the churches. He had reference to factions and personal strife which bring bitterness and disharmony into church life.

It is shameful to realize that the relations between these people demanded such strong words. Whereas love should prevail among Christians, there was warfare and pitched battles. Some have questioned whether such a low moral level could have arisen as early as the date which has been suggested for the writing of this letter. While this may seem unlikely to some, we need to remember that there was greed and strife even in the Jerusalem church (Acts 5).

This strife was wrong. It was wrong because it showed a complete disregard for the personality of the other individual. It was wrong because it indicated a total misunderstanding of God. It was wrong because it was unworthy of the Christ whom these people claimed to love and serve. Jesus said, "Blessed are the peacemakers" (Matt. 5:9). These people were not making peace. Instead, they were the active doers of wrong and injustice to others.

But why do such things happen in the life of any person, especially a Christian? James's answer is that they arise "out of your passions which are at war in your members." The word translated "passions" can more accurately be translated pleasure, but in the New Testament it refers to evil. It "does not necessarily mean sensual pleasures but that which is sweet and leads to sinful strife (like ambition, love of money or power)." [2] The passions differ in different persons and bring these persons into conflict as they seek to fulfil their passions.

Wrong Methods in Seeking Gain

There is nothing basically wrong with desire. It may be either good or evil. Every person has desires of some sort. The important thing is that these desires be kept under the control of the Spirit of God. They must be worthy desires, and they must be sought in the right way. One of the difficulties of the people to whom James wrote was that they sought to fulfil their desires improperly.

Verse 2 has received a variety of translations. "Ye lust, and have not: ye kill, and desire to have, and cannot obtain: ye fight and war, yet ye have not, because ye ask not" (KJV). The difficulty in this translation is the statement "ye kill, and desire to have." It seems strange that the desire to have, or coveting, follows killing or murder. Ordinarily you would expect the order to be reversed. (Moffatt changes the verb "kill" to "envy." "You crave, and miss what you want: you envy and covet, but you cannot acquire: you wrangle and fight—you miss what you want because you do not ask God for it.") Remembering that the earliest manuscripts had no punctuation, it seems likely that the best translation of this verse would be: "You desire and do not have—you kill. You covet and are not able to obtain—you fight and wage war. You do not have because you do not ask." The writer seemed to want his readers to know that they were not necessarily wrong in their wanting, but in the way they sought to obtain their desires. They should have asked God.

Thus, the killing and fighting result when men are unable to obtain their desires in other and more legitimate ways. How modern all of this sounds. "You desire and do not have—you kill." Stories with this theme regularly appear in the daily newspapers.

---

[2] Robertson, *op. cit.,* p. 143.

Murder is not an unusual occurrence. Human nature has not changed during the past two thousand years. Men are still caught up in the same web of sin which has plagued man through the centuries. We may not like the idea of sin, and many try to deny its reality; but the evidence of its presence is all about us. What do men do when they cannot fulfil their desires through lawful means? As a last resort they turn to murder. For too many in this age, human life is cheap and is not allowed to stand in the way when passions seek fulfilment.

The second part of James's statement repeats and emphasizes the first. "You are not able to obtain—you fight and wage war." Bitter strife occupied members of the churches. They could not achieve their wishes in any other way than in rivalry and disorder. This should not happen with Christian communities, but it did in those days and it does in our own day. More than one church has been divided because of the strife stirred up by some individual who was more concerned to gain his own selfish ends than he was in preserving and strengthening the fellowship of believers. Church splits, while sometimes used by God to further his purposes, are the result of the selfishness, the ambition, and the desires of men.

James said that the reason these people did not gain what they sought was because they did not ask. He remembered the teaching of Jesus concerning prayer. "Ask and it will be given to you; seek and you will find; knock and it will be opened to you. For everyone who asks receives, and he who seeks finds, and to him who knocks it will be opened" (Matt. 7:7-8). Of course, this is not a blanket promise indicating that one will receive anything for which he asks. God never makes such a promise. The asking must be according to the will and purpose of God. God will not give us anything which we want to use for selfish purposes. He will not give us anything which will be harmful to us, but James knew that God is the giver of all things. If we are men and women of faith, then we must go to God to seek the fulfilment of our proper desires.

Wrong Motives in Seeking Gain

But what about those who did ask God and still never received what they desired? All prayers were not answered then according to the expectations of the worshiper any more than they are today. Does this mean that God is not concerned and that he does not give to his people? Of course not! It means that in many instances the individual has asked from the wrong motivation. "You ask and you do not receive because you ask for the wrong purposes, in order that you may spend it in your passions." Two different verb forms of "asking" are used. The contrast between the two implies that the first form is the mere use of words without the true spirit of prayer. One translator has it: "You ask with the lips and receive no answer, because you do not ask with the heart" (Mayor). They spoke but they did not pray.

It does no good to ask God from a wrong motivation. God will not give when we ask for the wrong thing, but we may sometimes ask for the right thing and still not receive because of the wrong motive behind our prayer. Jesus was also concerned with the matter of motivation (Matt. 5:21-48).

What was wrong with the motives of the people to whom James referred? They wanted to spend ("consume," KJV) what they received in the fulfilment of their passions. They were selfish in their desires. The verb "to spend" is the same one found in the story of the prodigal son (Luke 15:14). It was also used in the instructions to Paul to pay the expenses of certain Jews who were undergoing purification rites in the Temple (Acts 21:24). The term can be used to refer both to wise and wasteful expenditure. In this instance, of course, James was thinking of wasting their possessions just as the prodigal son had done. In all of this we are reminded that while God is gracious and generous, we need not expect him to give those things which we do not need and those things which we intend to misuse.

AGAINST FRIENDSHIP WITH THE WORLD (4:4)

The desire for material possessions and gain constitutes a dangerous and deadly friendship with the world. James recognized that the world was aligned in opposition to God. He warned that people could not be loyal to both God and the world. There has always been a tendency to attempt to be in the good graces of God and at the same time remain friendly with the world. All too frequently we hear the instruction of being in the world but not of the world as though it were stated: Be in the world and be of the world.

James harshly reprimanded those who sought to maintain a neutral position between the world and God: "adulteresses" is the term he used. The text from which the King James Version was translated reads, "Adulterers and adulteresses." Copyists took the term literally and felt that James must have addressed the men as well as the women. Therefore, they added the masculine term. Some commentators have felt that the feminine term should be taken literally, stating that such a condition as James was concerned with must have been due to the wickedness and active cooperation of the women. This would account for James's making specific accusation against them.

However, it is more likely that the term should be taken as a figurative expression. In the Old Testament there are places where the people of Israel are looked upon as the bride of God (Isa. 54:5; Jer. 3:20; Hos. 2:16). When they were unfaithful to God, they were accused of committing spiritual adultery. This seems to be James's idea. Christians are the bride of Christ (John 3:29; 2 Cor. 11:2; Rev. 19:7). Therefore, any disloyalty to him would constitute adultery and would bring the deserved accusation—"adulteresses."

The demand for a choice was no new one. The same type of decision was required of God's people in the Old Testament. The prophets came calling the people back from their worship of false gods to the one true God. Jesus demanded that people must choose between God and things. "You cannot serve God and mammon" (Matt. 6:24). John stated: "Stop loving the world and the things in the world. If anyone loves the world, love for the Father is not in him" (1 John 2:15).

In James, the term "world" is not used to refer to the created order, the world of men and things. It is not used simply to refer to those things which are visible. Instead, it refers to all that is opposed to God and his rule. This is why Christians must be careful about their attitude toward all that is about them. When Jesus prayed for his disciples (John 17), he prayed that they might be kept from devotion to the world. They were not of the world, but Jesus sent them into the world just as the Father sent him into the world (John 17:18). Thus, while we live in the created world and our service is performed in this world, we must never allow ourselves to become a part of the world, a part of that which is enmity toward God.

We are so accustomed to having our lives controlled by or built around the things of the world that the words of James appear quite strange to us. Yet Satan uses the things of the world to tempt and allure men into unfaithfulness to God. When we begin to take a genuine interest in these things, it is easy and seemingly almost inevitable that before long they have first place in our lives.

Some of these things that become enmity to God may be good in and of themselves. Money and a good paying job are important in the life of a husband and father. He needs these to provide proper care for his family, but this job and the money he earns may become more important than his relationship and service to God. The baby born into the home of young parents is a wonderful delight and blessing, but the young parents may become so wrapped up in that child and its welfare that their loyalty to Christ takes second place and tends to be forgotten. Examples could be multiplied, but these should be sufficient to remind us of the danger that we face. "Friendship toward the world is enmity toward God."

"Therefore whoever wishes to be a friend to the world is constituted an enemy toward God." The same word, "is constituted," was used in 3:6: "The tongue is constituted an unrighteous world in our members." Man does not need to be an enemy of God. He makes himself such by placing the world at the center of his life instead of placing God there. And God is a jealous God who will not share his love with any other person or thing. He must be given first place or the individual is completely estranged from him.

AGAINST PRIDE (4:5–10)

James had something to say to every man when he warned that God opposes the proud. Lest we be prone to think of pride as the sin of which some other person is guilty, let us be sure we understand the word. The Greek used in James 4:6 is a combination of two words meaning appearing above others, showing oneself above others, appearing to be superior to others. Pride can creep into our thinking without our intending it to do so. We are caught in its grasp without any real struggle on our part. Pride takes many forms. It may be pride in our heritage, our material possessions, our physical attractiveness, our education, our occupation, or any of numerous other things. It may even be a pride in religious matters. We are proud because we are Christians and others are not. We are proud of the position we hold in the church. Pride erects a barrier between the individual and God. Such pride can easily creep into our relationships at work, in our church fellowship, and in social contacts. This is why James warned against this trait and called his readers back to repentance and humility before God.

Jealous Yearning by God

"Jealously God yearns for the spirit which he has made to dwell in us." The general content of the verse is in agreement with several passages of the Old Testament, although it is impossible to be certain which ones James may have had in mind. Some have suggested that the reference to Scripture was merely looking forward to the quotation from Proverbs 3:34 to be found in the next verse. However, this seems unlikely.

Usually New Testament writers were quite accurate in their quotations from Old Testament literature, but sometimes the New Testament quotation does not agree exactly with any version of the Old Testament which we have. This might be because they used a version which has since been lost. Many times it was because they were quoting from memory. On other occasions, and James 4:5 is one of them, the quotation does not closely resemble any single passage in the Old Testament. Yet James introduced it with the usual words of citation from the Old Testament, "the scripture says."

"Further, the translation of the Authorized Version is difficult: 'The spirit that dwelleth in us lusteth to envy.' Taken that way, the sentence seems to be a condemnation of the human spirit, but that translation is hardly possibly. There are two possible translations, which in the end give much the same sense. 'He [that is, God] jealously yearns for the devotion of the spirit which He has made to dwell within us,' or, 'The Spirit which God has made to dwell within us jealously yearns for the full devotion of our hearts.'

"In either case the meaning is that God is the jealous lover, who will brook no rival, and who will share the human heart with no other love. The Old Testament was never afraid to apply the word *jealous* to God. Moses says of God to the people: 'They provoked Him to jealousy with strange gods' [Deut. 32:16]. He hears God say, 'They have moved me to jealousy with that which is not God' [Deut. 32:21]. . . . *Jealous* comes from the Greek word *zēlos,* and *zēlos* has in it the idea of hot and burning heat. The idea is that God loves men with such a passion that He cannot bear any rival love within the hearts of men." [3]

Note how God's jealousy differs from man's. When a man is jealous, it causes intense suspicion, anger, and hurt. But our jealous God "gives more grace." This grace is given us that we might accomplish the complete surrender God yearns for from us. The key to receiving this grace is in our humility. "God sets Himself against the proud man, the man who fancies that he is conspicuous beyond others, . . . so that the proud man has a formidable foe indeed, whereas to the humble God comes with reviving grace [Psalm 138:6; Isa. 57:15], with exalting grace [v. 10]." [4]

Therefore, we have no reason to be puffed up. All of us have been guilty of sin. None of us has done anything to deserve salvation. It is all the free gift of God, and only when we accept it as such do we truly become his children. The only way to true honor is through such humility. Peter said, "Therefore, humble yourselves under the mighty hand of God in order that he may exalt you at the proper time" (1 Peter 5:6).

Submission to God

Humility must show itself in complete submission to God. This is at the heart of Christianity. Any faith that does not produce this is a false faith, the kind which James has earlier referred to as a dead and barren faith. At the same time, this is one of the most difficult qualities that any of us is ever called upon to manifest. We desire to be independent. We are taught to make our

[3] William Barclay, THE LETTERS OF JAMES AND PETER (Philadelphia: Westminster Press, 1958), pp. 122–23.
[4] *Ibid.,* p. 79.

own way; and the idea of dependence, even upon God, goes against all that we feel to be an essential part of our being. We are determined to be equal to or above all others. Therefore, we do not want to be submissive to anyone.

This pride is the most vicious of Satan's tools used to keep us from loyalty to God. We are much like Simon Peter. He recognized Jesus to be the Messiah, but he sought to instruct Jesus as to what the Messiah was to do and be (Matt. 16:13–23). We desire the forgiveness of our sins through Christ. We want him to be our Saviour, but then we act as though we have absolute authority over our lives and know better how they should be controlled than does God. Beyond the desire for the forgiveness of sin, there is little willingness on our part to be submissive. James would remind us of this essential quality of life. His words serve as a warning to us when we are tempted to place ourselves in opposition to the will of God. The proper and safe course for every Christian is to be yielded to the control of God in every detail of life.

Resistance to the Devil

A part of this submission to God expresses itself in an active resistance to the allurements of Satan. It is foolish for us so seldom to be submissive to God and so frequently to be submissive to the devil. Common sense, as well as religious experience, should teach us that the opposite should be our practice. Sin has so infected our lives and so confused our minds and weakened our wills that our sense of values and our loyalties have been reversed. It seems so simple to understand: God is our creator and redeemer; Satan is the one who would utterly destroy us and replace all good with evil. In spite of such simple logic, we forget that as God's people we are to resist Satan.

God provides the strength necessary for any individual who would resist the working of Satan. James reminded his readers to submit themselves to God. Herein is the strength for resistance. What is needed is the willingness to resist. And the Christian himself must supply the willingness; God does not coerce his children. And when there is no resistance, Satan gets his way. We need to combine the help of God with our own willingness to resist the wiles of the devil. Paul gave assurance to the Christians at Corinth: "God is faithful, who will not permit you to be tempted beyond what you are able, but with the temptation he will give you a way of escape . . . that you may endure it" (1 Cor. 10:13).

Perhaps our problem is that we hesitate to oppose an enemy that we cannot see. We recognize that the devil is powerful, and we fear we may lose the battle. But James gave assurance that if we oppose the devil he will flee from us. No matter how strong he may be under certain circumstances, when we, in the power of God, stand against him, the devil becomes a coward and flees the scene of battle. We need not fear. In simple trust and humility before God, we can be confident that God will give the victory to those who put aside selfish interests and pride and submit themselves completely to his leadership.

Approach to God

The only way man can be victorious over Satan is through the cleansing which comes by repentance and worship of God. So James encouraged his readers: "Draw near to God and he will draw near to you." This does not mean that the initiative belongs to man. Jesus' words remain true: "You did not choose me but I chose you" (John 15:16). But James indicated that God permits himself to do only so much. He has limited himself in his creation of man. He never forces any man to a decision against his own will. God has done all that he can do in the gift of his Son and in the presence of the Holy Spirit. Man must respond to that. He must draw near to God, and when he does so he discovers that God is there, drawing near to him.

The word James used is one which carries the idea of approaching God to worship him. It is used of the priests as they prepared to undertake their responsibilities in the Temple. It is used also of all worshipers. (See Heb. 7:19.) Evidently James was implying more than merely a casual approach to God. Man comes as a worshiper; he draws near in recognition of God's holiness and power, and gives himself completely to this God in adoration and service.

One difficulty is that many people are not in the proper condition to so approach God. Our God is a holy God. He cannot tolerate sin in those who would come near to him. Therefore, James admonished, "Cleanse your hands, sinners, and purify your hearts, you double-minded men." James was true both to the Old Testament and to the teaching of Jesus in this command. The psalmist said: "Who shall ascend the hill of the Lord? And who shall stand in his holy place? He who has clean hands and a pure heart" (Psalm 24:3-4, RSV). Jesus said: "Blessed are the pure in heart, for they shall see God" (Matt. 5:8).

The reference to clean hands had a literal significance for the Jew with his idea of ceremonial purity. For the Christian it takes on a figurative meaning and refers to the forgiveness of sin and the attempt to live a righteous life. It emphasizes the outward conduct of life, while the purity of heart stresses the inward relationship of the individual to God. James would never have separated the two aspects of religion. His emphasis all along has been that the inner life and its outward expression are inseparably bound together.

The reference to the double-minded takes us back to 1:8 where James referred to people who could not make up their minds whether to trust God or not. Such indecision prevents them from drawing near to God. Before they can do so, they must purify their hearts and put their trust in God without reservation.

Another aspect of this call to cleansing and repentance is found in the demand in verse 9: "Be wretched and mourn and weep. Your laughter is to be turned into mourning and your joy into dejection" ("heaviness," KJV). The word translated "be wretched" appears only here in the New Testament. Paul used a related word as he cried out, "I am a wretched man" (Rom. 7:24). "Wretched" carries the idea of one who has come to realize his own weakness and inadequacy before God. The recognition of personal inadequacy must bring mourning and weeping. The realization of condemnation before God must be a cause of concern for the one who is truly repentant. Jesus' teaching in the Sermon on the Mount again comes to mind. "Blessed are the poor in spirit, for the kingdom of heaven is theirs. Blessed are they who mourn, for they will be comforted" (Matt. 5:3-4).

Those things which from an earthly point of view brought laughter now bring grief. The things which brought joy now bring sorrow. The total outlook on life is changed when a man comes to God. This is the experience of the converted sinner. James indicated that those who had begun to love the world needed to be brought back to a full realization of their need of a changed outlook toward the world. The wrong things were bringing joy. They needed to gain a correct evaluation of life.

Humility Before God

Once more, and for the final time, in verse 10 James called upon his readers to humble themselves before God. Humility is the direct opposite of pride. To humble ourselves before God means we must admit that we have nothing upon which to rely in the presence of God. Our best is worthless before him. Our few good deeds are meaningless because of our sin. In the final analysis, we must rely totally upon God's mercy.

The result of such humility is that we will be lifted up or exalted. This means that God will accept us as though we were worthy. He will accept us because of our faith and trust in him.

In salvation and Christian growth, there is no room for reliance upon self, only for reliance upon what God has done in Jesus Christ.

We must be careful that we do not attempt to humble ourselves in order that God may exalt us. In fact, if this is our motive, it is extremely doubtful that there can be any true humility. We must never seek status or position for ourselves. When we do, we lose sight of the proper relation which should prevail between ourselves and God. He must be first and we are only his inadequate servants. Any status to which he exalts us is due to his mercy and not something which we have earned. James was not encouraging an attempt to gain position by the false approach of a pretended humility. Our yielding to God must be real. There can be no sham and no pretense. If we could do away with such false humility today, a vast change might be worked in our lives and in the ministry of our churches.

AGAINST SLANDER (4:11–12)

One of the most vicious ways of building up self is to tear down someone else, and the most efficient way of doing that is through the use of words. So James once more returned to the matter of speech. He had already made several references to it (1:19,26; 3:1–12). In these two verses he dealt with one aspect of it, the matter of speaking evil against others. This is another step beyond the warning against cursing men. There are many who would never pronounce a curse on anyone but who would not hesitate to slander or speak evil against someone if it served their purposes.

Tremendous harm is done by the spoken word. The command has always been, in effect, that we are not to slander. " 'You shall not go up and down as a slanderer among your people' " (Lev. 19:16, RSV). This is one of the requirements of God that is most frequently violated. Certainly the leaders of Judaism continually spoke against Jesus during his ministry. Christians have always been tempted to speak against one another and against outsiders.

Such destructive talk is wrong because "he who speaks against his brother or judges his brother speaks against the law and judges the law." It is quite likely that the law to which James referred is the same royal law to which he had reference in 2:8. This royal law is the law of love. We cannot speak evil against an individual and love that person, and the Christian must always be guided by love. All our words and actions must be evaluated against the background of love. Anything which does not meet the requirements of love must be avoided.

James's statement that we become judges of the law when we judge our brother means that when we intentionally violate any law we are saying that it is a bad law and should not be a law. This places us in the category of those who make laws rather than obey them. This is disastrous in any organized society. Even with the imperfections of men and the consequent imperfection of human law, civil laws are to be respected. The attitude of being a lawgiver, rather than one who obeys law, leads to anarchy. A nation is thrown into confusion and chaos by such an attitude. This tendency to flaunt the law brings mob rule and the idea that might makes right. Under such circumstances, all true law ceases to be reality.

If it is true that disrespect for civil law leads to chaos, imagine the consequences when such an attitude is applied to God's commandments. There is no imperfection in his laws. They are not unjust or unfair. To seek to judge his laws means that we think we are wiser than he. To seek to replace his laws would mean that we consider ourselves to be greater than God. This is the basis of sin and idolatry.

There is great danger in such a simple thing as speaking against someone else. Malicious talk is definitely wrong. Even gossip is not an innocent item which we pass on for the sheer delight of it. We must consider every statement that we make to determine whether or not it is true and whether or not it helps instead of harms, for we have the responsibility to build up, not to tear down. God is the supreme Lawgiver and the supreme Judge. He is the only one "who is able to save and to destroy." In the light of the greatness of God and his mercy to all, "Who are you, you who judge your neighbor?"

Jesus' words are pertinent at this point. "Do not judge lest you be judged; and with the judgment by which you judge you will be judged, and with the measure by which you measure you will be measured" (Matt. 7:1–2). Jesus was concerned because men are able to see sin in the lives of others and, yet, fail to recognize it in their own lives. But more is involved here than this failure. Not only were those to whom James first wrote keenly aware of sin in the lives of others, they were condemning those in whom they saw sin. This is closely related to James's idea of speaking against a brother. Even if what we say is true, it may still be wrong to say it if it brings harm instead of good.

James did not overemphasize control of speech. Speaking out in a judgmental way does more harm to Christian fellowship than any other act. If we speak, it must be in love and with an awareness that God alone is in a position to judge.

AGAINST FALSE SELF-CONFIDENCE (4:13–17)

The final warning James issued was against those who thought it was within their ability to do anything they chose to do. Man is continually making this mistake; he has illusions of omnipotence. The more power he controls, the greater the danger will be that he will err in this way. No age of man more than our own has offered a greater temptation to believe that all power is in man's hands.

Planning Without God

The picture in these verses is of the merchant planning his strategy for the future. James would not have considered advance planning to be wrong. The fault of these merchants was that they were doing their planning without taking God into consideration. They remind us of the farmer whom Jesus condemned as a fool because he was interested only in his own material gain and did not consider the will of God in his life. "Fool, this night they will demand back your life from you. To whom will these things belong which you have prepared? Thus is he who stores up for himself and is not rich toward God" (Luke 12:20–21). It is never safe to leave God out of our plans and considerations.

"Come now," repeated in 5:1, is a challenge to the self-confident planners to consider seriously their situation and take stock of what they are doing. It is well to plan to go to a specific city and stay for a time, but these men were only seeking gain through their greed. They would go and stay as long as the market would permit. When they had fleeced the people, they would move on to another city. Their one purpose was to "trade and get gain."

Those persons, so arrogant in their self-reliance, needed to realize that they knew nothing about tomorrow. The future is always cloaked in mystery. They did not even know whether there would be a future. How did they know they could stay in that city for a year? Perhaps their lives would be taken from them before that time had passed. Far more important for them was that they give attention to what God expected and demanded of them. Only in the light of that did they dare make any plans for the future. This is still true for us. "For you are a mist that appears for a little while and then disappears."

The idea of life as a mist or smoke or vapor is a common one in ancient literature. It emphasizes the fact that life is brief and uncertain. It is here today but there is no assurance of tomorrow. Life must be lived in that realization. Therefore, James has suggested that we should say, "If the Lord wills, we shall both live and do this or that." This is a wise caution; but, at the same time, it has become a slick phrase with little meaning for many of us who use it. We say, "If the Lord wills," but too often these words do not reflect the condition of the mind and will. The mere repetition of words will not suffice at this point any more than the repetition of the words "in the name of Jesus" will guarantee the answer to prayer.

James was seeking to impress upon his readers that they must always plan in the light of the will and purpose of God. In this respect conditions have not changed. The future is still uncertain. Life is still transient. We must plan in the light of God's will and purpose. Only then can we have assurance of completion.

Boasting in Arrogance

It is only a short step from self-confidence to arrogance. The person who feels he has only himself to consider in making plans is arrogant and exalts himself above others and even above God. Such was the situation of the people James was considering: "But now you glory in your arrogance." They had reached the point where their pride had become supreme. They thought there was no one who could do anything to thwart their plans. Not even God could overcome them. Therefore, they "rejoiced" (KJV) or "boasted" (RSV) in their position.

James called his readers back to the realization that such boasting or glorying is evil. If we could convince ourselves, in actual practice as well as in verbal assent, that God is supreme and there is no room for boasting before him, our lives would be quite different. Not even Abraham had a basis for boasting before God (Rom. 4:1-2). If he did not, surely we must realize that we have no cause for pride. We are not above God. We are still subject to him, and any one of us who is arrogant about his own life and his relationship with God stands in the position of a fool.

Sinning by Omission

The sins of which we are guilty do not happen because we do not know better. All of us know to do better than we do. We are continually guilty of doing those things which we know to be wrong, and quite often we are filled with remorse for the evil things we do and say. But we are not nearly so concerned about the sins of omission, about the good and positive things we left undone. We allow ourselves to be victim of the fallacious idea that as long as we do not do anything bad we are not guilty of sin. We fail to take into consideration that sins of omission are also evil in God's sight.

James said: "To him who knows to do good and does not do it, it is sin." Every one of us stands condemned by this statement. We are continually failing God by omitting to do what should be done. These people knew they should take God into consideration in their planning, but they failed to do so. Therefore, it was sin. We know we should take knowledge of God's will and consider it in all of our plans, but we frequently fail to do so. And when we do not, we are guilty of sin.

There are unlimited ways by which we are condemned by the statement in verse 17. The opportunity comes to speak our witness to the love and power of Christ, but we refuse. Occasions arise for us to render service in our churches, but we find excuses for not doing so. We are aware of social injustices, and we refuse "to rock the boat." We see little children and the elderly and disabled in physical need and we clutch our wallets more tightly. We see one lonely and discouraged because he is not "in," and we turn our backs so that we will not have to *see* him. We hear unfair and untrue words spoken, and we remain silent. We see our government, our country, our churches headed away from what seems to be God's revealed will, and we refuse to get involved. When we know what we ought to do but refuse to do it, for us it is sin.

The warnings James has given throughout this chapter set a

serious tone for us. We see ourselves doing the things against which warnings have been issued. We seek personal gain and advancement, sometimes by improper means and for unworthy motives. We are so much a part of the world (those things that are opposed to God) that we are friends of the world, even when it means we are unfaithful to God. We are proud and often speak against our fellowman. But perhaps nowhere are we more guilty of sin than at this point of omitting to do what we know God would have us to do. We cannot justify our omissions. No excuse will be accepted by God. We will stand before him not only to give an account of what we have done, but also to give an account of what we have failed to do. The words of Jesus once more stand as a witness against us when he pointed out that our failure to serve others is at the same time a failure to serve him. We will be judged as much by what we have failed to do as by what we have done (Matt. 25:41–46). We need to hear and heed James's call to repentance and humility before God.

7.
The
Individual,
Responsible
Before
God

The closing chapter of James's letter relates to a variety of topics centering around the individual's personal responsibility to God. To some extent, this has been true throughout the letter, but this emphasis appears in a special way in chapter 5. Of course, James did not lose sight of the outward aspects of religion, and these receive their due emphasis in this chapter.

At the close of chapter 4, James gave some warnings to those who make the mistake of planning without taking God into consideration. It was only a step further to write about the rich who ignore God and transgress against his standards and commands.

JUDGMENT OF THE RICH (5:1–6)

Were the rich to whom James referred members of the Christian congregations? They have been mentioned several times, and we have been forced to rely on the context of each passage for the answer to that question. The rich man referred to in 1:10 probably was a Christian. There is no way to be sure about the rich man in 2:2—all we can say is that he was a stranger in the congregation. Harsh things were said about the rich man in 2:6–7, and it is unlikely that he was a Christian. The merchants referred to in 4:13–17 may have been Christians, for it sometimes happens that the one who claims Christ may forget him in the conduct of his business. This should not be, but we know that it does happen.

It is extremely difficult to imagine that James was thinking of rich members of the churches as he wrote the stern words of chapter 5. Some question why words referring to outsiders were included in a writing addressed to believers. This is in keeping with the prophetic tradition where many times the prophet spoke to Israel God's word concerning those outside Israel. James's inclusion of such words of judgment in his epistle to Christians also served as a warning to any in the churches who might be tempted to follow the pattern of the rich.

Nature of the Judgment

James called on the rich to give attention to his words: "Come now." This was a summons to consider their position. James called upon the rich to weep and howl. These were signs of great distress, and this distress was the result of the miseries which were coming upon them. James was undoubtedly thinking of the final judgment of God upon these people who showed their separation from him by the manner of their lives. He used the word for "wail" that means even more than to wail; it means to shriek and depicts the frantic terror that will come upon those on whom the judgment of God falls. The tragic events which occurred in relation to the fall of Jerusalem in A.D. 70 are not necessarily ruled out. But primarily James was speaking of the wrath that is stored up for the day of God's wrath. That day is coming, and its misery will be beyond description.

Riches in James's day were measured in food, wearing apparel, and money (vv. 2–3). James insisted that the riches upon which these men were depending would prove to be inadequate and temporary. First, he pointed out that their riches would be rotted ("corrupted," KJV). Grain can be stored for only a limited time. After that it is unusable because it is rotten.

Garments are susceptible to the activity of moths. These garments in which the rich prided themselves and which constituted their wealth would become worthless because they would be eaten by moths.

Even money, which might be thought of as more permanent than either food or apparel, would be "rusted" ("cankered," KJV). Of course, gold and silver do not actually rust. The picture here is of the man who buries his money in the ground and when he goes to dig it up, finds it has become crusted over so that its value is hidden by the sediment deposited upon it. Money that is hoarded instead of used for good loses its value and becomes a curse to the one who possesses it.

Wealth in James's day and in ours proves to be false security for those persons who put their trust in riches rather than in God. Surely God's judgment will reveal to such persons that not only will their wealth not stand them in good stead, rather it will be used in judgment against them. "Their rust will be evidence against you and will eat your flesh like fire" (v. 3, RSV).

James gives us a vivid and frightening picture of the fate of those who hoard for themselves treasures here on earth. They give no thought to the future when these earthly things must vanish and be left behind. They do not heed the command of Jesus given in Matthew 6:19–20, in which he mentioned rust, moth, and thieves. Certainly James was aware of this teaching of Jesus when he gave his harsh warning. He did not mention thieves as Jesus did. He was concerned with the nature of material riches themselves rather than forces that might act from the outside. These things in themselves were false hopes and to treasure them meant alienation from God.

In these verses, James spoke of the last days. The "last days" in Jewish thought referred to the time of judgment by God, the days of the Messiah. The early Christians believed that they were living in the last days. The last days had dawned in Jesus' ministry. But James was looking beyond his day to the terrible judgment that would come in the final judgment. He warned that though the rich have the luxuries of life now, these luxuries will perish. What a tragedy it will be when the unrighteous rich discover that all of life has been based on the wrong things.

Reasons for the Judgment

James listed three evidences of the greed and injustice of the rich. They withheld the wages of the laborers in their fields; they lived a life of pleasure and indulgence; and they were guilty of killing the righteous.

In a day when wages are paid weekly or monthly, we have difficulty visualizing the situation that prevailed in the first century. It was exceedingly important that wages be paid to laborers at the close of each day's work, and this was the regular custom (Matt. 20:1–16). The laborer was dependent upon his daily wage to provide food for himself and his family. If he were not paid at the close of the day, he and his family would have to go to bed hungry that night. Therefore, it was clearly commanded in the law that the wages must be paid each day. (See Lev. 19:13; Deut. 24:14–15.)

The men condemned by James were wealthy landowners. They hired men with the promise of a day's wage, but at the close of the day they refused to pay it. The worker could do nothing; there was no way by which he could force the dishonest landowner to pay the wage. Since he depended on each day's wages for that day's food, all he could do was go home and go to bed without his meal. There was no excuse for such treatment of the worker. God was aware of this sin, for the wages that were withheld "cry out against you." James would have the rich to know that the laborers might go to bed hungry, but God knew their condition. He heard their cries, and he would punish those who mistreated them. The man who cheats in the conduct of his business affairs can expect no mercy at the hands of a righteous God.

The expression "Lord of hosts" ("Lord of sabaoth," KJV) occurs only twice in the New Testament, although it is common in the Old Testament. It pictures God as the Commander of the armies of heaven. The realization of God's power should strike terror in the heart of any man who would oppress those who cannot help themselves.

The second complaint James made was against the wanton indulgence of the rich. They lived luxuriously and in wastefulness. They went beyond what could be justified under any conditions; they flaunted their riches and wasted them in excesses. Israel had been plagued by such people in almost every generation. Prophets like Amos cried out against such luxury when the poor were starving. This matter raises a question concerning ourselves. Most of us are not rich, but we have an abundance of the necessities of life. Will God overlook our unconcern for the multitudes of people in our world who lack the minimum food and clothing needed for survival?

James said of the wasteful rich: "You have fattened your hearts in a day of slaughter." The imagery here is of an animal waiting to be killed, eating away without concern for what is to happen to it. Men can be so caught up in the luxuries of life that they lose all sense of values. Such persons tend to feel they have all the good that life can offer, and they fail to realize that this merely makes them suitable for slaughter. The end of such a life is destruction.

The third sin James mentioned is that the unrighteous rich condemned and killed the righteous man. There is much disagreement about James's exact reference here. Some commentators are convinced this is a reference to the death of Jesus. Jesus was referred to as the Righteous One and the Jews were accused of killing him (Acts 3:14–15; 7:52). The added statement, "he does not resist you," is looked upon as support for this view, for Jesus did not resist those who had decided to kill him.

However, it is more likely that James used the term "righteous man" in a more general sense. The Jews outside of Palestine could not be accused of killing Jesus. Paul was careful in dealing with Jews outside of Jerusalem so as not to condemn them for killing Jesus. This crime was the responsibility of those in Jerusalem, but the people in the areas to which this letter was addressed were often guilty of killing those who were righteous. The godly men, those who pleased God, were the righteous. Frequently, they were poor and defenseless. They were easy prey for the greedy and oppressive, and such greedy men would not shrink from committing murder in order to accomplish their ends.

James warned of a dark future for men guilty of such crimes. They could be sure that God would not forget, and they could know that they would bear the just punishment for their sins.

James spoke clearly to the readers of his day. He sounded a warning that ultimately riches are worthless, and he pointed to the disgusting traits of many who were rich. Surely the Holy Spirit would have James to write at least as sternly to our day— perhaps even more sternly. We live in a day when the question "How much was he worth?" can only be answered satisfactorily in material terms. Perhaps not even in Amos' day was there a clearer division between the haves and the have-nots. One has only to visit the inner city of almost any city in America to observe this truth—or stand by at lunch hour in many city schools!

Walk down the main street of your city and watch the faces and listen to the conversation of business and professional people. Sit alone at a restaurant table on your lunch hour and eavesdrop a bit. Materialism is the order of the day. Labor was forced to organize to secure its rights. Management now often finds itself at the mercy of greedy employees. Both groups lose sight of the supreme worth of persons and of the transitory nature of material wealth.

Landlords are guilty of depriving the poor of suitable living conditions in order to make a higher profit on their investment. Merchants use for their own gain the inability of the poor either to pay cash or to exercise a greater choice in their limited buying power because of inadequate transportation.

Unscrupulous businessmen prey on the restlessness and weakness of men to advance the sale of alcohol or to involve such persons in gambling. Day after day the ignorance of some groups provides an easy mark for scheming con men who attempt to get rich quick.

To all these persons in 1970, James would say, "Now, you rich people, listen to me! Weep and wail over the miseries that are coming upon you! Your riches have rotted away, and your clothes have been eaten by moths" (vv. 1–2, TEV).

But wait—before you feel relieved that James was not speaking to you. One may have the motives of the rich without his money. He may have the greed of the rich without his gain. Let us take care that we do not make ourselves "fat for the day of slaughter."

NECESSITY OF PATIENCE (5:7–11)

James condemned the rich landowners and those who lived in luxury without concern for the poor and the righteous. He called upon the faithful brethren to be patient and long-suffering. Although they were being oppressed and were suffering at the hands of the rich, he had a word of hope and encouragement for them.

Reasons for Patience

James urged his readers to be patient. This could be translated more appropriately, "Be long-suffering." Patience here is not simply waiting for something but having the willingness *to endure* that which is difficult and hard to bear. " 'Patience' is the self-restraint which does not too hastily seek vengeance for a wrong, while 'endurance' is the temper which does not easily succumb under suffering." [1] James was interested in the endurance of his brethren.

One reason why the readers could endure their difficult circumstances was that the Lord was coming. James spoke of the *parousia* of the Lord. The word used here was frequently used to refer to the return of Christ (Matt. 24:3,27; 1 Cor. 15:23; 1 Thess. 4:15; 5:23; 2 Peter 1:16; 3:4; 1 John 2:28). Such widespread usage emphasizes that Christians were eagerly expecting and awaiting the return of Christ. They were confident that the events connected with the death and resurrection of Jesus proved the triumphant power of God. The victory over evil had been guaranteed by what took place at the resurrection of our Lord. The return of Christ would be the consummation of that victory. Therefore, existing evil was really insignificant in comparison to the great joy which would be theirs when Christ returned. While Christians sought to change evil conditions, they were willing to trust God and believe that he would make things right, if not in this life, certainly in the life to come.

However, we must not make the mistake of thinking that these people were only concerned about the coming life. James, along with other New Testament writers, was vitally concerned with the present life. However, this present life can only be rightly understood, interpreted, and lived when it is seen in the light of the life which is to come.

---

[1] Ross, *op. cit.*, p. 92.

Some of James's readers were anxious for signs of the coming of the Lord. James did not give any evidence to show it was near. Instead, he encouraged his readers to have faith. He called their attention to the work of the farmer. Two things were essential for a good crop. The early rains must come in the late fall and soften the ground to receive the seed and cause it to sprout. But the farmer also had to await the late rains of the spring. These brought the harvest to maturity. If either the early or the late rains failed to come, there would be no harvest. The farmer could only do his work assuming that the rains would come. If they did not, it would be a long, dismal, and hungry year. If the rains came, he would have a good harvest.

The farmer could not hurry the harvest. It came in its due time. He had to endure the long period of waiting, sometimes under trying conditions. So it was with the believers to whom James wrote. The Lord would come! They could be confident of this. Because of this certainty, they could endure any trials and hardships that might come their way. "Strengthen your hearts, because the coming of the Lord has drawn near."

Nineteen centuries have passed and the return of Christ has not occurred. Does this mean that James and the other early Christians were mistaken? No, it simply indicates that the time is known only to God and that God's way of reckoning time differs from man's. The return could occur at any moment, and the true believer must live and act in the realization that the "coming of the Lord has drawn near." This confidence must guide every activity. We must live each moment with the quality of life that would be suitable were it the last moment. We must make every plan with the realization that the Lord could return at any time. We will then have assurance that God is in control and that victory belongs to him and his people.

James was trying to convey to his readers a deep and abiding assurance that God has ultimate control of history. This is the assurance that is needed in our world of strife and chaos. Whatever the hardship, if we have the power of God's Spirit within and the confidence of the return of Christ, we can be victorious over all that we encounter. "Strengthen your hearts." This is no time for fear and weakness. It is a time for courage, a time to go into the world to all men with the gospel of salvation through Jesus Christ.

The people to whom James wrote were guilty of inward bickering and accusations. We can identify with that situation. When things go wrong and we become discouraged and disillusioned, we look around for someone on whom we may place the blame. Most often we are careful not to blame ourselves. We feel we must find someone else who can share the blame. This is a dangerous habit to fall into for it nullifies Christian growth and activity.

The word James used for "grudge" or "grumble" in verse 9 means to sigh or to groan. The "grumbling" (RSV) is inward and unexpressed. Therefore, it is often unknown and, consequently, difficult to overcome. There is no room for such accusation against one another in the Christian fellowship. Even if the circumstances which must be endured are the fault of some fellow believer, the Christian must be forgiving. Jesus emphasized this need of forgiveness. Even among his disciples there was an unwillingness to forgive—how like us this is. One of the most difficult traits of character to develop is that of a forgiving spirit. We are quick to accuse others, but we are slow to forgive them.

Accusation inevitably leads to judgment, for it is itself a form of judgment. James earlier warned against judging our brother (4:11). When we set ourselves up as judges, we face judgment. We need to realize that only God is in a position to pronounce judgment. We are not to grumble or complain. Our task is to endure with the proper spirit, seeking always to do that which is God's will in our lives.

Examples of Patience

James liked to use examples. When he wanted to put the relation between faith and works in proper focus, he cited the examples of Abraham and Rahab (2:20–25). In order to emphasize the value of endurance, he cited the prophets and Job.

"As an example of suffering and patience, brethren, take the prophets who spoke in the name of the Lord" (v. 10, RSV). James did not specify any particular prophet. He knew that suffering had been a part of the life of almost every one of these men. The role of a prophet, a spokesman for God, is never a popular one and never a safe one from a human point of view. The world, as James used the word, is opposed to God; and those who follow the way of the world are opposed to God and God's spokesmen. The prophets had to take their stand against the popular opinions of their day.

They "spoke in the name of the Lord." They spoke on the authority of God and as representing God personally. Therefore, what the prophet said was not to be denied or rejected. His was not a human message; it was divine. As such, it was seldom pleasant and often provoked anger and physical abuse. This was true of the Old Testament prophets. It was likewise true of Jesus. He suffered affliction and had to endure all manner of opposition. The same thing was true of John the Baptist and the early followers of Jesus. As God's spokesmen, their message was opposed to the world and by the world.

Those who suffered as prophets would probably tell us that it was all worthwhile. We ourselves recognize that the judgment of the world is not the definitive answer. In fact, God often reverses the world's judgment. He did so with the prophets just as he did with Jesus. Those who are obedient to God are the ones who are called happy.

James also referred to an example of steadfastness. The term translated "patience" (KJV) really means steadfastness. It is the same term translated endurance in the previous sentence. Steadfastness is the quality that Job exhibited in suffering.

Job was not really patient in the ordinary sense of the term. In fact, "patience is far too passive a word. There is a sense in which Job was anything but patient. As we read the tremendous drama of his life, we see him passionately resenting what has come upon him, passionately questioning the conventional and orthodox arguments of his so-called friends, passionately agonizing over the terrible thought that God might have forgotten and forsaken him. There are few men who have spoken such passionate words as Job spoke. But the great fact about Job is that in spite of all his torrent of questionings, and in spite of the agonizing questions which tore at his heart, he never lost his faith in God. . . . The very greatness of Job lies in the fact that in spite of everything which tore at his heart, he never lost his grip on faith and his grip on God. Job's is no grovelling, passive, unquestioning submission; Job struggled and questioned, and sometimes even defied, but the flame of faith was never extinguished in his heart." [2]

Such steadfastness is what James was seeking to encourage in his readers. Even in the fact of oppression by the rich, or from whatever source hardship may come, the Christian must remain steadfast in his trust in God. Such steadfastness is the sign of true Christian faith. It looks at the ultimate outcome. Job could not look back and dwell on what he had lost. He could not even look at the present with the physical suffering which he endured. He was faced with the necessity of looking to the future. He had to see "the end of the Lord" (KJV). He had to believe that out of all that was happening, God would accomplish his divine purpose. His faith was that God would not leave him helpless, and his faith was vindicated.

From our vantage point in history, we can see the purpose of

---

[2] Barclay, op. cit., pp. 147–48.

God in what happened to Job. This should encourage us to see that God can work good in even the most trying difficulties. But he can work this good only when we are steadfast in faith and refuse to turn our back on him. "The Lord is full of compassion and mercy" declared the psalmist who had learned that God is truly a God of mercy and grace (Psalms 103:8; 111:4). Because we have the support of so great a God, we can bear anything which the world brings upon us. We are his, and nothing can separate us from him. "Therefore, brethren, be long-suffering."

PROHIBITION OF OATHS (5:12)

Throughout the letter of James, there are repeated references to sins relating to speech. At this point in his epistle, James also spoke out against taking oaths. The swearing of oaths was common among the Jews. Oaths were taken to guarantee the truth of what was said and the performance of that which was promised. Unfortunately, the swearing of an oath did not always guarantee these things, for the Jews distinguished between oaths. An oath sworn by something holy was binding—any other oath was not. Furthermore, taking an oath was such a common practice that many entered into these oaths lightly. They also profaned the name of God by glibly using his name to strengthen weak or false oaths. This practice had been condemned by Jesus (Matt. 23:16–22). Jesus also considered that it should not be necessary for his followers to swear (Matt. 5:34–37). Their word itself should be binding. Undoubtedly this statement of Jesus in the Sermon on the Mount was the background for James's command.

Two basic issues arise. The first, and more important, is that the Christian should have the reputation of always speaking the truth. An oath is to give assurance that what is said is true. James's readers would have felt that the individual might lie sometimes; but when he put himself on oath, he was giving assurance that he was speaking the truth. Jesus taught, and James echoed his words, that the believer should not have to give his oath. People should recognize that a Christian always speaks the truth. Even in the lightest moments what he says is true, and everyone knows it. When he says yes, that is exactly what he means. When he says no, that is binding upon him.

Such straightforward honesty should be the situation in dealing with a Christian. Yet all of us realize it is not always so. Unfortunately, many Christians have no better reputation for speaking the truth than does an unbeliever. In many areas, the word of a Christian is not trusted any more than that of any other person. This condition has grown out of sad and bitter experience. The Christian does not always pay his bills; he does not always keep his vows; he does not always stand behind his promises. Therefore, society makes the same demands on him that it does on others when assurance is needed. We have no one to blame but ourselves.

The second issue has received far more attention. Most people who refer to the teaching of James in the matter of taking oaths, or to the teaching of Jesus, try to apply it to the legal procedure in the courtroom or to the swearing in procedure for a government official. Is it proper for a Christian to take an oath under such circumstances? There has been much heat created in the discussion of this question. No answer would satisfy everyone concerned.

It is quite likely that in this instance James was not thinking of formal and legal oaths. Probably he was concerned about the oaths which were such a common part of the everyday life of these people. These oaths were wrong. They showed an irreverence for God and a failure to take into consideration his greatness and holiness. The Bible points out that God put himself on oath (Psalm 110:4; Heb. 5:6). Jesus allowed himself to be put on oath in his trial before the Sanhedrin (Matt. 26:63). Therefore, it would appear that swearing to tell the truth in court or swearing to honestly and properly fulfil an office would not be a violation of the command of James. These are matters of legal procedure.

One further point should be noted. Is this a warning against the practice of cursing as we know it today? Directly, it is not. Indirectly, the teaching of this verse can be applied, for cursing involves taking the name of the Lord lightly and irreverently. Taking an oath in the name of God with no intention of keeping it was taking the name of God lightly and dishonoring it. While cursing as we know it was not the sin of which James's first readers were guilty, his injunction can be of assistance in seeking to curb this unhealthy habit, found even in the lives of some church members.

ENCOURAGEMENT TO PRAYER (5:13–18)

Prayer is a good and positive way of using God's name. We call upon him reverently in prayer. James had some practical advice for his readers with regard to prayer. Earlier in the letter he had encouraged his people to ask God for wisdom if they lacked it (1:5). But there are other areas of life where prayer is more effective.

Occasions for Prayer

James wrote of three situations in which the personal relationship of the believer with God should be expressed. We are admonished to pray *when someone is suffering*. This is a broader term than sickness. It is the same word used in verse 10 to refer to the prophets who suffered affliction. Believers were subject to the same type of physical suffering as were men of old. This could have been suffering brought on by the political authorities. It could have been triggered by the social conditions of the time, even oppression by the rich.

The important thing is what to do when suffering comes. One might sit back and complain, or he might seek to remedy the situation by his own strength and ingenuity. James said: "He is to pray." The person who suffers must realize the power and mercy of God. He must submit his case into the hands of a God who judges righteously and trust that this God will either change the conditions or give him the strength to endure. This was what Job did. Paul faced and endured similar circumstances with his "thorn in the flesh" (2 Cor. 12:7–9).

Suffering is as great today as it has ever been in the history of mankind. While we have devised so many things to ease the afflictions of men, suffering still comes to untold millions of people. None of us is exempt. What are we to do when it comes? We are to pray.

The second occasion for turning to God is in the case of good cheer. *When a person is cheerful,* "let him sing praises" (RSV). He recognizes that what brings good cheer comes from God. Every good gift comes from him (1:17). The natural result of a cheerful heart should be praise to God.

It is a sad commentary upon human nature that we often neglect the singing, praising aspect of our relationship with God. We are quick to call upon him when trouble comes. In sickness or disaster, there is no hesitation in calling upon God. The term "fox-hole religion" expresses this tendency. In time of personal distress, we want the assurance that God is present to deliver us; but when everything is going well, we are not so aware of God. Pride can make us believe that we are responsible for the good that comes our way. We may be cheerful and rejoice with family and friends, forgetting that God is the giver of all good things. It is just as important for us to sing our praises to God in times of joy as it is to turn to him in times of difficulty.

The song of praise arises out of a condition of the inward man. Such singing need not be audible to the human ear. One can sing praise to God in his heart. There are occasions when it is proper that our song be audible only to God, but there are also many occasions when praise should be offered openly.

James also called upon his readers to *pray in times of sickness.* It is true that sickness is one aspect of suffering. Perhaps James separated it from other suffering because he had some specific suggestions to make as to what should be done when someone within the fellowship is ill.

Prayer of Intercession

No doubt James expected the sick man to pray for himself, but he was to do more. He was to summon the elders of the church. In all probability these elders were the official leaders of the church. In many respects they would correspond to our office of pastor. The term "elder" was derived from Judaism just as much of the organization of the church was somewhat like that in the Jewish synagogue. From what we can learn from the New Testament, each church had several elders. Their duties are never clearly defined. This passage indicates that part of their responsibility was to minister to the needs of the sick.

The elders were to be called, and they were to pray over the sick person and anoint him with oil in the name of the Lord. This stresses the importance of the prayer of intercession. These men were not praying for themselves; they were praying for their sick brother. One of the great experiences that any individual can have is prayer for someone else. Such prayer should be a large part of the prayer ministry of every Christian. We find it in the life of Jesus. We see it in Paul's prayers as recorded in his writings. We know it to be true in the lives of great Christians throughout the ages. James encouraged prayers of intercession on behalf of the sick.

Verse 14 indicates that James and his readers had faith that God is able to heal sickness. This should not be surprising to us. It was a common idea among the Jews. In fact, they went even further and considered that all sickness was the result of sin and, therefore, only God could heal. Jesus did not agree that all sick-

ness was the result of sin, but healing was a major aspect of his
ministry. The gift of healing was given to some of his followers,
and Paul spoke of the gift of healing as one of the gifts of the
Spirit (1 Cor. 12:9).

However, there is no suggestion in this passage that James considered that these elders had any particular gift of healing. They
were not the ones who healed the man. It was God who did so.
But their prayers were effective in the healing situation. We may
not understand how prayer works; but we know that when God's
people pray in faith and in submission to his will, prayers are
answered, even in the healing of physical disease. God heals—
and prayer is an essential ingredient in the process of healing.

The elders were to pray, and they were to anoint the sick with
oil in the name of the Lord. Some commentators interpret this
in the light of practice several centuries later when anointing with
oil became a sacramental part of church life. There seems to be
no reason for thinking of James's instruction in that light. Oil
was one of the two chief medicines of the first century. (The other
was wine.) Therefore, the elders were instructed to give religious
and medical help, prayer and oil. James realized there is no healing in which God does not have a part. Applying the principle
inherent in this truth, we can understand that doctors and medicine are a gift from God. When someone is ill, he is to pray and
get the best doctor and medicine available.

Whenever this passage is read, the problem is inevitably raised
concerning the faith healers who have received so much attention
in recent years. Does James have a word concerning our attitude
toward them? It may be impossible for any of us to give a definite
conclusion concerning the work of these men and women. It can
be said, however, that if healing does take place through the
ministry of these people, it is God who does the healing and the
credit should be given to God and not to men.

James pointed out: "The prayer of faith will save the sick man and the Lord will raise him up; and if he has committed sins, they will be forgiven him." This statement has two parts. The first undoubtedly refers to the healing of the man's body. The word "save" is frequently used in this respect in the New Testament. Of course, it also is used many times to refer to the individual's relationship with God and the forgiveness of sin. But James used it here to mean physical healing. He said that when prayer is offered in faith God will bring healing. He did not mean that every sick person will thus be healed. Obviously, this did not happen then and does not happen now. It does mean that when healing can be fitted into God's purpose, then God will honor the prayers of his faithful people by healing the sick person.

The second part of James's statement in verse 15 concerns the sick man's spiritual condition. How is this related to healing? Some interpret the verse with the realization that the Jews believed that disease was the result of sin. Therefore, in order for a man to be healed, his sin had to be forgiven (Mark 2:1–12; John 9:1–3). Thus, to the Jew, the fact that the man's illness had been cured indicated that God had forgiven his sins. Another possible understanding of this statement is that the realization that God had brought the healing would lead the healed person to repent of his sins and ask God for forgiveness and, therefore, receive that forgiveness. It is impossible to be sure which of these is what James meant. The former would make good sense assuming the Jewish viewpoint toward sin and sickness, but the latter interpretation is more in keeping with Christian concepts. It is God who both forgives our iniquities and heals our diseases.

Prayer of Confession

The reference to the forgiveness of sin led James to a third important aspect of prayer, the prayer of confession. We are well aware of the need of confessing our sins. The prophets called on the people of Israel to confess their sins to God that he might forgive them. Jesus demanded confession and repentance, and his disciples through the centuries have insisted that men must confess to God that they are sinners.

But James, while agreeing that sin must be confessed to God, wrote here of confessing our sins "to one another." He realized that for proper relationships to prevail within the Christian community there must be a humility that brings recognition of sin and a willingness to confess sin that it might be forgiven. This does not sanction an indiscriminate confessing of all our faults to anyone who will listen. Not every person needs to know all about the life of any one of us. But there is healing value in having someone to whom we can go and discuss our weaknesses and temptations, knowing the concern of that person and that he will join us in prayer that these sins may be avoided. There are times when an individual will need to make confession of sin to the church, when his sin has been an offense against the church and a cause of harm to the fellowship of the church. Only then can Christian relationships be restored.

This passage does not support the idea of confession to any individual with the idea that he can communicate God's forgiveness of individual sin. This idea finds no support in James or anywhere else in the New Testament. Confession to others can bring the healing of human relations, but each of us must confess to God to receive his forgiveness and to maintain unbroken fellowship with God.

The outcome of confession to one another should be prayer for one another. Unless this is the result, there may be little point in confession. But when our fellow Christians, in sympathy not condemnation, understand our situations and pray for us, there is available a source of strength that cannot be measured. Note that a tremendous responsibility rests upon those who hear the confession.

One reason why confession to one another is little practiced is because of the fear, frequently justified, that others will condemn and ridicule us if we confess our sins to them. Also, we may feel that we cannot trust them to keep our confidence. If we could be assured of understanding, sympathy, concern, and love, we would be much more willing to follow James's teaching at this point. So there is need for improvement on both sides. The one who has sinned needs to feel the value of confession; the one who hears the confession must do so with a Christian attitude and response.

Power of Prayer

How effective is prayer? How great is its power? James said: "The energized supplication of a righteous man avails much." The word translated energized is that from which we get our word "energy." It emphasizes the operating power of the petition. The prayer is active and really accomplishes something, but it must be the prayer of a righteous man. Sin in the life means that prayer cannot have its full effect. Can this be the reason why sometimes we feel our prayers are not effective?

Once more an example is given. This time it is Elijah. Here was a man whose prayers were heard and answered. Lest anyone think it was because of something peculiar about the makeup of Elijah, James pointed out that Elijah was similar in nature to every other man. He was of "like passions" with us. Therefore, if God heard and answered his prayers, he will also hear and answer our prayers when they are offered in the same spirit as those of Elijah.

James stated that Elijah prayed earnestly or fervently that it not rain, and it did not rain for three and one-half years. The Old Testament does not say specifically that this was the prayer of Elijah. The prophet told Ahab: " 'As the Lord the God of Israel lives, before whom I stand, there shall be neither dew nor rain these years, except by my word' " (1 Kings 17:1, RSV). Some feel that the expression, "before whom I stand," should be interpreted as an indication of prayer, but we cannot be certain about this. Jewish tradition, which James may well have been following at this point, understood the drought to be the result of Elijah's prayer. It is true that the Old Testament gives the impression that the drought may have ended in the third year (1 Kings 18:1) instead of in three years and six months as Elijah prophesied. The difference may simply be in the way in which time was counted.

Actually the time element was unimportant to James because his emphasis was upon the effect of Elijah's prayer. He prayed and no rain came. He prayed again, and the rains came in abundance. If the prayer of a man can be so effective in controlling the weather, certainly God's people should not be hesitant in prayer concerning the things which are of significance in their lives. Prayer has power beyond the highest imagination of man.

RESTORATION OF THE STRAYING (5:19–20)

The final brief section of the letter of James is one of the most difficult passages to interpret. There is great uncertainty about part of verse 20.

James seems to be writing about a Christian who turns away from the true faith. "My brethren, if anyone among you strays from the truth and anyone causes him to return, know that you who caused the sinner to return out of his straying way will save his soul from death and will cover a multitude of sins." (The King James Version uses the word "convert," but since this term has a particular meaning for us in bringing the lost person to a saving experience with Christ, it is better to use some other term to refer to the return of the straying church member.)

What did James mean when he said that the one who brings him back "will save his soul from death"? To whom does "his soul" refer? While some think this means that the one who restores the straying individual receives forgiveness for a multitude of his own sins, this seems contradictory to all that we find elsewhere in the New Testament. We do not earn merit by leading back those who stray. We help them because we share the love of God for them. Therefore, it is best to take this as a reference to the person who has strayed. When he is returned to the fellowship and repents of his sins and confesses them to God, God will forgive. His spiritual life will be healed (this is the same term as used in v. 15 with regard to the healing of the sick), and his sins will be covered. They will be covered from God's sight, and they will also be covered as far as his fellow believers are concerned. These sins will not be held up as a constant reminder of his past weakness or as rebuke to him. Rather, Christians will share the attitude of God and rejoice that the one who had strayed has returned to the fellowship.

CONCLUSION

James brought his letter to an abrupt close. There is nothing in the ending that resembles the ordinary letter. There is not even a benediction. This is typical of a writing which was so intensely practical. (Compare the close of Proverbs.) There is nothing to distract our attention and cause us to forget the great demands which have been made upon us.

James was not concerned about theological discussions. He was concerned with the practical outworking of faith. This caused his writing to be virtually overlooked by many generations. But it may be that today there is a crying need for us to return to the practical matters of which he wrote if we are to meet the needs of people in our world. We dare not neglect what he said. With the help of God, we need to put into practice the Christianity which he so effectively set forth. It is hoped that the brief study that has been made of this letter will lead to such results in the lives of the people who engage in this study. If it does, our lives, our churches, and our communities will be blessed.

Personal Learning Activities

The answers to the following questions may be found by a close reading of the book of James and each chapter of the study course book.

Chapter 1 *(Fill in blanks.)*

1. The author of the letter gave his name as _____.

2. The most probable date of the letter is _____.

3. The readers were probably _____ _____.

4. The writer was quite familiar with the Jewish _____ literature, including the book of _____ in the Old Testament.

5. The writer was well acquainted with the teachings of Jesus, especially the _____ _____ _____ _____.

6. The purpose of the letter of James was to convince the readers that their _____ must be shown by their _____.

Chapter 2 *(Match a statement on left with a word or phrase on right.)*

7. ____ The source of wisdom
8. ____ The source of temptation
9. ____ The results of trial
10. ____ The results of yielding to temptation
11. ____ Attitude toward trials
12. ____ Reward for endurance
13. ____ Blessings given by God

a. Endurance and maturity
b. The crown of life
c. God
d. Good gifts, faithfulness, and new birth
e. Our own desire
f. Sin and death
g. Joy

Chapter 3

14. List the three qualities which help to work the righteousness of God.

15. List the two aspects of true religion.

16. List the evils of partiality.

17. List the chief characteristics of the hearer of the Word and of the doer of the Word.

18. What is the "royal law"?

Chapter 4 (*In the space provided write the letter corresponding to the correct answer.*)

19. ____ In writing about the relation of faith and works, James

    a. agreed with Paul in every detail.

    b. completely contradicted all Paul said.

    c. wrote about a different aspect of the relationship.

20. ____ James referred the quotation "Abraham believed God, and it was accounted to him for righteousness" to

    a. the sacrifice of Isaac by Abraham.

    b. the promise of a son to Abraham.

    c. the promise of the land to Abraham.

21. ____ In writing about faith and works, James was primarily concerned to show

    a. that a man is saved by works.

    b. that works are of no significance.

    c. that true faith must show itself in good works.

22. ____ James said that faith without works is

    a. weak.

    b. dead.

    c. adequate.

Chapter 5 (*Fill in blanks.*)

23. The discussion of the abuse of the tongue was directed mainly toward Christian _____.

24. Some were desiring to be teachers because of _____ _____.

25. The examples of the importance of small things were the _____ in the mouth of the _____ and the _____ of the _____.

26. Teachers face a _____ _____ because of their great responsibility.

27. The tongue was likened to a _____.

28. The man who completely controls his tongue is called a _____ man.

29. False wisdom was described as _____, _____, and _____.

30. List the results of true wisdom.

Chapter 6

31. List the five areas of spiritual failure against which James warned.

32. List the three evidences of false self-confidence.

33. List the things which James suggested will help to overcome pride.

Chapter 7

34. The three things which constituted wealth in the first-century world were _____, _____, and _____.

35. What reasons did James give that the rich were subject to punishment?

36. As examples of patience, James cited _____ and the _____.

37. Three occasions which should be met with prayer are _____, _____, and _____.

38. The two types of assistance to be sought when ill are _____ and _____.

SUGGESTED AUDIOVISUAL MATERIALS

Chapter 1

FILMSTRIP: *The Epistle of James,* 50 frames, color, recording

Chapter 2

MOTION PICTURES: *More Than Conquerors,* 30 minutes; *To Walk in Faith,* 30 minutes, color

Chapter 3

FILMSTRIPS: *The Christian Life,* 52 frames, color; *A Church Ministering,* 50 frames, color, recording

Chapter 4

FILMSTRIPS: *Discussion Starter, No. 4,* 46 frames, color, recording; *Abraham, Man of Faith,* 27 frames, color, recording

Chapter 5

MOTION PICTURE: *My Will Be Done,* 30 minutes, color

Chapter 7

MOTION PICTURE: *The Rich Fool,* 28 minutes
FILMSTRIP: *Teach Us to Pray,* 38 frames, color, recording

BIBLIOGRAPHY

Colson, Howard P. *The Practical Message of James.* Nashville: Broadman Press, 1969.
Chitwood, Billy J. *Faith Plus Works.* Nashville: Broadman Press, 1969.

Erdman, Charles R. *The General Epistles.* Philadelphia: Westminster Press, 1918.

Mitton, C. Leslie. *The Epistle of James.* Grand Rapids: William B. Eerdmans Publishing Company, 1966.

Robertson, Archibald Thomas. *Studies in the Epistle of James.* Nashville: Broadman Press, 1959.

Ross, Alexander. *The Epistles of James and John.* William B. Eerdmans Publishing Company, 1954.

Tasker, Randolph Vincent Greenwood. *The General Epistles of James.* William B. Eerdmans Publishing Company, 1957.

* The listing of these books does not imply endorsement of their total contents by author or publishers of THE LETTER OF JAMES.

The NEW Church Study Course

The New Church Study Course effective in January 1970 is based on more than three years of study and design. It offers several improvements in the Church Study Course, which began in October 1959. At that time three courses previously promoted by the Sunday School Board were merged: the Sunday School Training Course, the Graded Training Union Study Course, and the Church Music Training Course. Principles and methods books of the Woman's Missionary Union and the Brotherhood Commission were added in October 1961 and January 1967 respectively.

The New Church Study Course offers increased flexibility in meeting the needs of Southern Baptists. It provides courses of varying length and difficulty, varied formats and types of course materials, additional types of credit, and improved organization of courses.

The New Church Study Course consists of two types of courses: the Christian Development Course for all church members, and the Christian Leadership Course for church leaders. Courses are organized into subject areas.

The purpose of the Christian Development Course is to provide courses of study which will help church members grow toward maturity in Christian living and competence in Christian service. These courses offer more comprehensive, advanced, and varied learning experiences in subject areas of a church's educational program than can be provided through curriculum periodicals. It also provides tests and exercises, credits, and diplomas of achievement which help church members measure their progress in developing needed knowledge, understanding, and skills. Units of instruction are provided for Preschoolers and Children. These are designed to reinforce foundational learnings. Materials which churches may use in recognizing the participation of Children in these units are available from Baptist Book Stores.

Christian Leadership Courses provide a comprehensive series of courses organized into subject areas dealing with knowledge, understandings, and skills needed for effective church leadership. Tests and exercises, credits and diplomas to help leaders measure their growth in leadership ability are included in some courses. The Christian Leadership Courses are the primary source for leadership training materials prepared by the agencies cooperating in the New Church Study Course.

Courses of both types are designed to be effective for individual and class study. Learning aids, study guides, and teaching guides are available for some courses. Credits are granted to Youth and Adults for reading, individual study, and class study.

The New Church Study Course is promoted by the Sunday School Board, 127 Ninth Avenue, North, Nashville, Tennessee 37203, through the departments in the Education Division; by the Woman's Missionary Union, 600 North Twentieth Street, Birmingham, Alabama 35203; by the Brotherhood Commission, 1548 Poplar Avenue, Memphis, Tennessee 38104; and by the respective departments in the state conventions affiliated with the Southern Baptist Convention.

A record of all credits and diplomas earned should be maintained in each church.

Detailed information about the course and the system of credits, diplomas, and record keeping is available from the agencies listed above.

Forms for keeping records may be ordered from any Baptist Book Store.

Requirements for Credit

This book is the text for course 3204 of subject area 2 of the Christian Development Course of the New Church Study Course. If credit is desired for this course through class study, individual study, or reading, the following requirements must be met:

I. Classwork

1. This course is designed for seven and one-half (7½) hours of class study and carries three credits for such usage. If the course is studied in a class setting of less than seven and one-half (7½) hours, the following criteria apply:
   (1) Five (5) class hours—two (2) credits
   (2) Two and one-half class hours—one (1) credit
   The teacher will indicate the length of the class and the number of credits to be granted on the Request for Course Credit (Form).

2. A class member who attends all class sessions and completes the reading of the book as directed by the teacher will not be required to do any written work for credit.

3. A class member who is absent from one or more sessions must complete the required exercises or questions in the "Personal Learning Activities" section on all chapters he misses. In such a case, he must turn in his paper by the date the teacher sets (usually within ten days following the last class). Also, he must certify that he has read the book.

4. The teacher should request an award for himself. A person who teaches a course for Youth or Adults (in any subject area) will be granted the same number of credits as class members. The teacher of an approved unit of study for Preschoolers and Children will be granted two credits in course 6299 in subject area 62. Request award by using Form 151.

5. The director of Training Union or the person designated by the church should complete the "Request for Course Credit" (Form 151) and forward it after completion of the class to the Church Study Course Awards Office, 127 Ninth Avenue, North, Nashville, Tennessee 37203.

II. Individual Study

1. A person who wishes to complete this course without attending class sessions may receive full credit by certifying that he has read the book and by completing all exercises or questions in the "Personal Learning Activities" section.

2. Students may find profit in studying the text together, but individual papers are required. Carbon copies or duplicates of the answers cannot be accepted.

3. The work required for individual study credit should be turned in for checking to the director of Training Union or the person designated by the church to administer the New Church Study Course. The form entitled "Request for Course Credit" (Form 151) must be used in requesting these awards. It is to be forwarded by the director of Training Union or the person designated by the church to the Church Study Course Awards Office, 127 Ninth Avenue, North, Nashville, Tennessee 37203.

III. Reading Credit

1. A person may receive one credit toward the diploma on which he is working by reading this book.

2. Upon completion of the reading, he must complete the "Request for Course Credit" (Form 151). He should give the completed form to the director of Training Union or to the person designated by his church to be responsible for administering the New Church Study Course.

3. The director of Training Union or the person designated by the church will see that the request is completed, signed, and forwarded to the Church Study Course Awards Office, 127 Ninth Avenue, North, Nashville, Tennessee 37203.

V. Awards and Records

Two copies of the course credit award form will be sent by the Study Course Awards Office to the church. One copy should be filed in the church training record and the other given to the individual.